WOMEN *In* SYNC

Secrets Every Woman Should Know

Suzanne Weinstein

Acknowledgements

This book is dedicated to the amazing women who strive for Being In Sync.

A special thank you to my mother for always supporting and encouraging me to realize that my only limitations in life are the ones I have placed on myself.

Permission:

Each author in this book has given the copyrights of their chapter to be used herein with their permission. Each author is responsible for the individual opinions expressed and statements made.

InSync
CONSULTING

Contact
Suzanne Weinstein
In Sync Consulting Corporation
InSyncConsulting.com
(888) 444-9141

Contents

My Declaration

I declare I am inspired to live more boldly in my knowing of myself in my truth. To love more deeply, with more compassion and understanding. To be more accepting of myself and of others. To know myself as safe and in service. To be courageous as knowing in all my choices.

Being In Sync One Moment At A Time,

Suzanne Weinstein

Introduction

Some people talk of the spiritual experience as an event or a particularly powerful experience that causes them to see things differently. My own spiritual journey has been more gradual, but it has included powerful experiences. Along the way I have met incredible people and learned lessons that altered my life path. This book, *Women In Sync*, was born from one of those powerful, life-changing experiences that allow one to see things differently.

As a child, I always felt a pull to go within. Some call people like these introverts. I was always at the extreme end of that scale. I was very shy, and rarely did I speak up or say much to those I didn't know. I often found myself observing others. As I watched them, I felt as though I was hearing their stories. Some I made up and some I believe to have been telepathic "hits," where I was actually able to pick up on the thoughts of those around me. I thought it was fun to see how different everyone was, and yet how we all had similar stories.

When I was about seven years old, I had my first conscious encounter with the spirit world. It was a frightening experience that was difficult to explain or understand. A man was trying to touch and feel me while I was lying in my bed. I didn't know what really happened because when I called for help, my mother searched the entire house, inside and out, but couldn't find the person that I absolutely knew I had seen, felt, and experienced. I didn't speak of this experience again until I began my spiritual journey as an adult trying to grasp my gifts of spiritual dimensions in a more practical way.

When I was accepted into graduate school, I thought, "Wow, they must let everyone in these days." I had creatively written a letter with my application stating that my undergraduate grades did not accurately reflect my aptitude for learning. While I was trying to project self-confidence and pure determination to change things in my life, I was in fact making excuses to myself for my perceived lack of worth. A life lesson that I would encounter over and over again as an adult: knowing our worth is key to our conscious development. I find self-worth to be a particularly troublesome area for women.

This self-worth issue wasn't one I thought the "outside" world could notice. However, as I learned that what is inside persists, I knew intuitively that I would have to change some things. What was it within me that needed to be transformed?

After receiving my degree in Organizational Leadership, I went into coaching and consulting work. I had always been one of the people who was sought out for advice. I developed strong skills in understanding human needs and loved my work, but I felt that something was missing. I wanted to have a greater impact on the organizations I worked with and the people who made them tick. Most of the senior executives I advised were men, and I started to notice that when I spoke, my comments would often cause them to physically move back. This happened repeatedly, and I recognized it as a pattern. Patterns being my area of expertise, I knew that there was something deeper going on.

I knew intuitively that my consultations were accurate, but I also knew that if people could not hear them, my time, energy, and efforts would be wasted. This brought me to a realization: If I could change my approach, that would influence how my information was received. Genius, right?

If I was going to have a greater impact, I would be able to do so only by changing me. I already thought I was pretty intelligent, aware, and intuitive—my ideas about my capability to do things were never an issue. However, modifying my approach could change the direction of my clients' paths. To be truly successful, I was going to have to change my mode of delivery and develop my feminine power.

Working to develop this power was more difficult than I ever would have imagined. I come from a strong family of independent women, and I was an alpha woman before they even had a term for it. Shy? Yes! Strong? Yes! Independent and wise? Absolutely! However, what I showed on the outside was somewhat different from how I felt about myself on the inside, and I wanted this to change. I believe that the inside is what creates our outside. Yet change from within is a painful experience. Looking back, I would have preferred running five back-to-back marathons to facing my weaknesses.

When I started my journey, I actually saw feminine power as a weakness. I didn't understand the true strength present within myself. I had to examine my judgments about women in a new light.

I had always been a person who loves the outdoors, so I spent time in nature to reflect. I enjoyed meditation, so I did an intense journey of guided meditation specifically around my feminine power and myself. From that experience, I started asking myself one question daily: How can I be more compassionate with myself? I knew that if I could find my compassion, become nurturing and caring toward myself, that would automatically change what I saw in the world and in my clients. I practiced this daily questioning for one full year. It was simple, and it worked to help change my life forever.

I continued with meditation and experimented to find what worked for me. I loved learning about other modes of self-reflection to find what was going on inside of me. I spent a significant amount of time working with a beautiful Sufi man, Navair, who showed me what letting go of the past could be like. His focus was specifically on Past Life Regression. This was an enjoyable, sometimes intense journey into my past to find out what I could release and let go of now.

This experience led me to try other healing modalities. Each healing taught me more and more about my true essence as a woman and as a healer of sorts myself. Hmm, could this be true?

As I started a new phase of my feminine power development, I wondered what my next step would be. This led me to the study of Peruvian shamanism. I would read and get scared, then read some more. I was drawn to people who would share a personal story about other people that I "just had to meet." When we talked, shamanism would come up. I really wasn't certain what a shaman healer was, but I was certainly intrigued.

As I learned more about shaman healers, I learned that often they utilize plant medicines in their work. One plant frequently used in ceremonies is called "aya" or ayahuasca, the Quechua word for "spirit." It is a powerful medicine based in feminine energy used historically by the indigenous people of the Amazon. As I read more and more about the plant and other people's experiences, everything about the ceremony and medicine attracted me. I knew this was my next step. I had to go to Peru. I also knew that in doing this, I would never be the same again. It seemed nuts and completely reasonable at the same time.

I signed up for the trip and then chickened out. I was not ready for the change that was coming. It was like dancing with the unknown, unsure whether you are going to like the beat of the song. I decided I would wait for a sign. The following year I had a painful breakup with a boyfriend and thought that was it: the sign to just go and be free once and for all. I thought to myself, "I am going, I am changing; I will face my fears and I will never be the same woman. It's time to go."

I booked my trip and went to Peru to work with a shaman who is known worldwide for his work with aya for over forty-seven years. I thought if I was going to do this, he was the one with the greatest experience and would have compassion for me. From what I had read, I was going to need as much compassion as a person could take. Working with the medicine is no joke!

The journey was arduous. After a long flight to Peru, then waiting at the airport overnight for a local flight, I was already exhausted by the time I took the boat ride out into the Amazon. Yet I could see right away that Peru is a magical country—words do not give the spirit of the land justice.

The ceremonies are fairly long, lasting between five and seven hours. I had gone to Peru for an experience of transformation, and during that time, every part of my being was challenged and transformed. My first night was filled with agonizing pain. I responded so strongly to the medicine that I purged for over seven hours straight. Paradoxically, it was also one of the most beautiful experiences of my life.

I woke up the next morning not fully understanding all my learning. I was sure that I had come into contact with a part of myself that I had been longing to know—that part of myself that longed to be filled with love and compassion. This is what I now believe to be the heart of every woman. I was filled from the inside and absolutely, completely immersed in love. It was a visceral feeling. I knew, without a shadow of a doubt, by the end of my trip that I was to develop this book and that I was destined to connect women with their own power in some way.

First and foremost, I learned that feminine power is to be embraced, not feared. That in sharing our collective experiences, we can learn and perhaps avoid some of the pitfalls and difficulties. That if we as a group of women share our advice and even one person is helped, we will have done something to shift our word to a better place.

I learned specifically that to be loving, nurturing, gracious, and compassionate is not a weakness, as I once thought, but a power. That as I create an environment for myself knowing that I am always surrounded by love, I can share that experience with others and perhaps they, too, will know this for themselves and be more courageous, confident, and generous with others. That is the purpose of this book. It is one step in the direction of learning to share our stories so that we can let them be teachers for ourselves as well as for others.

For me, a spiritual experience is a daily occurrence. It's an opportunity every day to embrace my knowing of who I am, what I am, and how I service this thing called life. Every day I am learning more and more to understand my worth. To share my knowledge and experience with others so that they may grow and, if they so choose, transform. Transformation is available to us all, and it happens through our connection with one another and ourselves. It's through knowing ourselves that we see the world. This book is an opportunity to learn from those who have walked before you and have something important to share. Each chapter was specifically written to share a piece of wisdom that we wish we would have known before. Every work written is a gift to help you learn of your own worth and your own knowing. It is with great love that I share this with you.

Leadership from Within
"Fears are as real as we believe them to be."
by Suzanne Weinstein, MA

Suzanne Weinstein has committed her life to the growth of visionary, authentic, and meaningful leadership. The founder of In Sync Consulting Corporation, she is an accomplished coach, strategist, and change management and transformation consultant. She lives in San Diego, California and regularly conducts seminars, workshops, and keynote speeches. Visit www.insyncconsulting.com for more information.

"Suzanne, did you bring your homework?" my professor in graduate school asked me in front of fellow master's and doctoral students.

"Yes, but I didn't do it exactly as you asked." Go figure. I've always been a little on the creative side. Some high-level research says that might be due to my learning disability. Whatever the reason, it doesn't generally earn you points when you are stuck in the academic system.

As always, I did a creative interpretation of the assignment. We, as a class, were asked to bring in a poem that we thought said a little bit about who we were. I was excited about this project. Finally I would get to know a little bit more about these people who sat beside me.

My grades in college weren't the strongest. Let's just say that a big part of my understanding of college was of the social aspect. Never in my wildest dreams would a girl like me ever go to graduate school. After all, I had severe dyslexia, and reading took much longer than the average. Not to mention I had a habit of creating different words as I read (a talent that I would keep to myself, until now.) My test scores, well, they were passing. As I was applying to graduate schools I added—yet another creative part on my end—a letter that explained very clearly that my college transcripts did not accurately reflect my aptitude for learning. *Ha!* Good, right? Somehow, it worked. I was on my way to being the first one in my family to attend graduate school.

I interrupted the professor as the class discussion continued. "Professor," I said. "When will we get to the poems?"

The professor answered, "I am not sure it is the right time."

Are you kidding me? I said in my head. I knew I was not going to be able to listen to the meaningless banter of the students. I had been really looking forward to hearing some poems and gaining an understanding of the people around me. I couldn't wait. Now I was being told that "the right time" wasn't here. *What?*

Before I knew it, I was interrupting the professor again, as she was allowing the students to meander (as I saw it). "Excuse me, Professor. I can't do this anymore. This talk of this and that seems meaningless to me. There are more important things we can talk about. Can we start with the poems, please?"

The class was dead silent. I thought to myself, *this is where I am found out. I wasn't supposed to be let in here.* I sat quietly, as the professor conversed openly with the teaching assistants in the room. Finally they agreed that maybe we should move forward.

"Suzanne, would you come to the front of the room and read what you brought?" the professor said to me.

"Well, I wasn't really thinking I would share mine. I was most interested in just moving forward."

The professor motioned her arm for me to come to the front of the room and stand before the class. I thought to myself, *at least I have on a perfect suit and look presentable.*

"Okay," I sighed as I maneuvered my way around the chairs. As I stood there in front of the class, I held my head high and kept my nerves together.

"Suzanne, I would like you to read the poem you brought."

What? I thought, *read? Read out loud, in front of others?* That was my biggest fear. I thought everyone would know how different I was now. They would know my weakness. I didn't want to do this. I was now standing in front of the class and I couldn't go back to my seat. Heck, I had already interrupted the class three times. Going back was not an option.

The day the assignment was made, I knew from the beginning what I wanted to share. I knew it was an expression of me in many ways. You see, my poem really wasn't a poem at all but a portion of a speech that I had heard one day and had posted in my apartment. It was given publicly by Nelson Mandela, the first black African to be named president of South Africa, a leader for whom I have much respect.

I took a deep breath and started my poem. I did my best to keep my nerves at bay and tried diligently to read what was actually on the paper instead of the creative mix my dyslexic mind sometimes puts in place. I thought I did pretty well and was looking forward to sitting back in my empty seat in the audience. I was finished. I had survived the reading.

My professor said I had read too fast and that she would like me to read the poem again. *What! Really?* (Sigh.) Okay. So I would read the poem again. This time it seemed almost fluid. I was impressed with myself, again thinking I'd done a pretty good job.

"That was good, Suzanne. Would you be willing to read it again? This time, I would like you to look at the class and read the next step as the class is ready to hear what you say." The professor was so nice and gentle as she made this request. I had such respect for her. Of course, I would read it again. In that moment I had to understand quickly what it meant to "read the poem as the class was ready to hear."

And so I read the poem again. This was the third time. I felt that I knew the words very well by now and was less nervous about reading correctly and more concerned with interpreting the directions correctly.

As I stood there looking at the eyes of my peers, it seemed every nerve in my body was on edge. I could hear a high buzz in my head and wondered what it was. I didn't have time for this. I needed to read with the "rhythm of the class," as I interpreted it. I took a deep breath and began my reading. Slowly and purposefully, I read each word of the poem.

As I did, the poem began to take on a new life. Each and every word was said purposefully and eloquently as I was gifting it to each student. It was a gift from me to them. As I got to the last part of the poem, I paused. My eyes welled with tears. I stood there, as I looked at these people who I thought were better than I was. I took a deep breath as a tear rolled down my face and said: "And as we let our own light shine, we unconsciously give other people permission to do the same. As we are liberated from our own fear, our presence automatically liberates others."

Great, now I was standing there and I was crying. This was not what I knew of leaders. They don't cry in public. They aren't vulnerable. They don't share their deepest thoughts and fears as I just did and still be respected.

The class applauded, as I think we all knew, at some level, that we had experienced something special. Something completely unexpected and magical had just occurred inside of me. I had done it! I had faced one of my biggest fears: of reading in front of people.

"Thank you, Suzanne," the professor said to me. "I have something else I would like you to try if you are willing." Without hesitation, I accepted. After all, what could possibly be harder or worse than what I had just done?

The professor said, "I would like you to sing a note, any note you choose, and sing it to the class."

I immediately went numb. *This lady is clearly out of her mind. Sing!?! I don't even sing in the shower. Sing in public? I don't even know what a musical note is. This is crazy.*

She briefly demonstrated. "AHHHHHH."

"Are you kidding me? I can't." I began to feel an attack of the nervous giggles. This was a different fear, and it was one I wasn't even aware I had moments ago.

There I stood in front of my peers, just having faced one of my biggest fears, and now this? I looked at the class. The nervous giggles took over me. Soon I realized I had to just do this. I took a few deep breaths, trying to calm myself. I opened my mouth wide in hopes something resembling a musical note would emerge. Nothing! I tried again—"AHHH"—and then it would stop. Again and again, nothing!

My final instructions were to look at the eyes of the students and when *I sensed* they were ready, let the note come out. These directions were clear. I was to go deep inside of me and then I would know I could sing.

The class was utterly silent. All eyes were on me. They were waiting for me to give them this musical note. I followed the directions and waited. I would look at the eyes of the students and they would look back. Holding their gaze, I could see them clearly, not just as people but as vibrating beings. The silence was held for a long period—I was later told it was more then 10 minutes—before I sensed the class was ready for my note.

Then, as I stood front and center, a tear rolled down my cheek, and out of the silence the note emerged from deep within me. A power surged as I released this big and bold "*ahhhhhhhhhhhhhhhhhhhhhhhh*." I held the "ah" for a prolonged period of time until I sensed that it was immersed in each student. In hindsight, it is still one of the most powerful learning experiences I have had in my life. I changed in those brief moments. I changed how I viewed people, groups, silence, sound, and most important, how I viewed me. This single experience changed the course of my life.

You see, often in our life we think we have to go it alone, do it ourselves, be strong, and never cry in public. I'd told myself a lie for many years, and now I knew that it was no longer the truth for me. I learned that the true sign of a good leader is one that allows others to be who they are and yet shows them that there is another way. Leaders emerge from those silences. They emerge from deep within each of us. We become great leaders from the inside out. It is not the clothes we wear or the image we portray that makes us stand out. When we embody courage and risk, and face our fears—this allows the leader we are meant to be to come forth.

Fears are as real as we believe them to be. They are allowed only the power that we give them. At any point in our lives we can choose to take our power back. We are the ones who can demolish our fears by standing in front of them and walking through them. When you do this, the gifts are undeniable, your inner strength will shine through, and your life will flow in a way you have never imagined. When you listen from within, you will lead in sync.

Happiness Is Having It All

"I've had enough experience with the male species to know that when a guy tells you something, listen— because he means it and he isn't going to change."

by Noel Alzua

Born and raised in Huntington Beach, California, Noel spends her time there living life and working as a marketing consultant. She has over 15 years of experience in the advertising industry, serving as an account manager and media planner for a number of Fortune 500 and privately owned companies. She holds a bachelor of arts degree in Communications from California State University, Fullerton.

At the end of a recent workout, my trainer said to the class, "Noel is the happiest person I have ever met. She's always laughing and smiling, and never complains." "Really?"I said in disbelief. But everyone agreed. How could this be? I definitely don't consider myself to be "sunny"and "cheerful"—especially when I'm getting my butt kicked by a personal trainer. When I think of happiness, Winnie-the-Pooh's annoyingly cheerful and bouncy pal Tigger is usually who comes to mind. For someone who has felt a lot more like Eeyore over the last few years, the compliment came as a surprise.

While I was a happy child and have enjoyed happy times in my adult life, it's been a long time since I've felt genuinely happy. And now, at the age of 39, divorced and virtually unemployed, what business do I have being happy? I definitely don't"have it all"—at least by American standards, where "having it all"usually consists of the following: a spouse, children, a career, a house in the suburbs, and lots of "stuff."

For a time, I was on my way to having it all. I thought marriage would make me happy, and it did for a while. In hindsight, I think I was happy because people weren't judging me anymore for not being married. Because in American society, no matter how successful you might be, if you're over 35 and single there must be something wrong with you. Once the "when are you going to have kids"or "when are you going to buy a house"started up, I again felt inadequate and pressured to live up to society's standards.

It's not that I didn't want children. During my marriage, I chose not to have a child because it turned out that my husband didn't really want children. While he never said it in those exact words, he did tell me not to expect him to change diapers or get up in the middle of the night. That made me pause and think. I've had enough experience with the male species to know that when a guy tells you something, listen—because he means it and he isn't going to change. I won't even get into the house issue, except to say I am old-fashioned when it comes to money and there was something fishy about everyone suddenly being able to afford million-dollar homes on the same income as ours. Once I accepted that we were probably not going to have kids or buy a house, the spotlight was on us as a couple. And once that happened, it became crystal clear to me that I wasn't happy. That was enough for me to know that I had to get out.

Not having a mortgage or children made divorce easier. I wouldn't say it was emotionally easy, but it wasn't financially or logistically complicated, and I was able to move on. However, it did mean that I was now even older and divorced, with no kids, no house. I felt like a complete failure, but I still had a career and I could support myself. And for that I have my mother to thank. From the time I was old enough to understand, she stressed the importance of education and career so that I would never have to rely on a man to support me. She'd known way too many women who stayed in bad marriages because they couldn't make it alone. Thanks to her, I had taking care of myself down to a science. That was no problem. I had moved in and out of countless apartments and paid my own bills for years. I had a secure job that I'd been at for 10 years, so I was fine. I was back on the quest to having it all.

At 37, I found myself with a great a guy who shared my values. The only thing still impeding my happiness was my career. Every single night I bitched about my job: *I'm disappointed in management. There is no order or structure. They hire the wrong people. My boss is passive-aggressive. I don't feel appreciated.* And all the while, the sound of my own voice bitching and complaining was slowly grating on my own nerves. I'd go to bed every night in a bad mood. And when I woke up, it would take every fabric of my being to pull myself out of bed, pin my tail on, and get my ass to work. I was officially Eeyore.

Through it all, I sucked it up and put on a happy face and did my job. I knew certain co-workers were very well aware of my unhappiness, because they were unhappy too. But a lot of us stayed at the job we didn't like, for whatever reason. For me, it was a combination of loyalty and fear. I'd been at the company for so long, and had many clients that I really liked and didn't want to let down. I loved the work itself and still strived to do my best. I was comfortable and scared of change. I'd had other offers, but I didn't have the self-confidence to leave and was petrified of failure. No matter how great everyone told me I was or how amazing I was at my job, I still lacked the confidence to move on. I was so used to the dysfunction and it had become so "normal" to me that I was afraid that other offices might be even crazier. At least I knew this crazy. The longer I stayed, the more trapped I became. During the last few months, every day felt like Groundhog Day, and I'd often IM the words "Kill Me" to my boyfriend.

On November 18, 2008, my boss did just that. Well, not exactly. But he killed "that" me. On that seemingly ordinary day, my boss called a meeting to discuss the future of the advertising agency. Many meetings that didn't bear good news had been called this way. I'd survived layoffs following 9/11, dealt with lost accounts, seen high employee turnover, and experienced reorganizations. I had been through it all. It was no secret that the economy was bad and that there were going to be more layoffs, but never in a million years did I think that I would be one of them. In fact, I was handling the bulk of the business. (Lesson: we're all expendable.)

But 10 minutes later, I was unceremoniously told the

following: "I am going to have to let you go, because we can't afford you anymore."I was given my last paycheck, a cardboard box, and sent on my way while others sat in the conference room staring in disbelief. And that was that. Despite the many years, and the many sacrifices I'd made for the sake of the company, my boss did not thank me for the work I had done or wish me good luck. I guess I should not have been surprised, but I was. Feeling as if I had been socked in the stomach and thrown out to pasture, I held my head high, walked out the door, and drove away in complete shock.

I'd been playing phone tag with another ad agency that wanted to meet me, so there was a chance that I was going to have another job soon. A colleague whom I'd been working with for a couple of years had recommended me for a position. She had become a friend, and knew that I wasn't happy or challenged anymore, so she'd started keeping her eyes open for me. I'd passed up some of the opportunities because I wasn't ready to leave, but this wasn't one of them.

Not long after, I met and interviewed with five different senior associates. It was a long hiring process, and I later learned that they were also stalling to make sure that budgets were intact and that new business was going to move forward before they hired me. After three months of interviewing and waiting, and interviewing and waiting some more, I got the job. My old boss even sent me a congratulatory email, which I accepted as his way of saying "thank you and good luck"after all.

It was scary starting over, but after a couple of weeks I felt totally at home. I was challenged and working with incredibly bright, talented individuals. There was no drama and everyone got along. It was almost too good to be true. And, just as I was settling into my new position, and my old job was becoming a fading memory, my new boss delivered some bad news. The agency's clients had drastically cut budgets, and new clients had just put work on hold indefinitely. And yes, there were going to be layoffs, and they would no longer be able to keep me.

"You've *got* to be kidding me!?!" was the first thought that popped into my head. I was surprised, to say the least. Yes, I was upset, but certainly nowhere near feeling the devastation I'd felt before. With that, I realized that I had already changed. It helped that my new boss reassured me that I was an asset by keeping me on as a consultant for the firm. There were other layoffs that day too, and the others were genuinely supportive even though I'd only known them a short while. I felt worse for them because I'd already been through it a few months earlier. I was now a veteran at being laid off.

The year 2009 was a tough one for a lot of us. Unemployment is the worst it has ever been in my lifetime, and the world has changed. And as the world has changed, my definition of "having it all" has changed. And oddly enough, I find myself the happiest I have ever been, and grateful for the things I have. I might not have a husband, but I do have someone who loves me. I don't have children, but I have friends and family. I don't own a home, but I am not homeless. I don't have a steady paycheck, but I am not in debt. I don't have health insurance, but I have my health.

I am both grateful and gracious. I am no longer in a huge hurry to get through the line at the supermarket, and

I let people go ahead of me. Not that I didn't do that before I lost my job, but now it really is a "no problem." I help other friends who are unemployed (or under-employed) with their jobs searches and encourage them on the days they are down. I listen to the birds sing in the morning, as opposed to telling them to shut up so I can get some more sleep. I enjoy my life, and find myself laughing and playing like I haven't done in years. And, I am grateful for the time and freedom to do so.

I guess there is a little Tigger in me after all.

Don't Worry… Be Happy

"Over 90 percent of people on this planet focus more on
what isn't working than they do on what is working or
what they want."

by Joanna Withey

*Joanna Withey is the creator of PlayfulLiving.com, an
online community for people who want to leverage the law of
attraction to create the life of their dreams and have tons of fun
doing it! Guided by the premise that life is supposed to be fun
and we can be, do, and have anything we want, Joanna has
studied with several brilliant spiritual teachers and noticed
that many people may listen to how they can change their lives
but very few actually take the steps to make it happen. That's
why she created Playful Living—to provide fun tools, products,
and support to people who desire a life full of fun and success.
To join any one of her 30-day challenges or contact Joanna
directly, visit www.PlayfulLiving.com.*

For most of my life, I've been the kind of person who
is very logical and realistic… observant of what is and is
not working well around me and always questioning how
things could be better. I used to care more about what other
people thought of me than I did about how I felt myself,

and I always seemed to give credit to what others thought was right for me instead of trusting my own intuition. Do you know anyone like that?

Over 90 percent of people on this planet focus more on what isn't working than they do on what is working or what they want. Think about it…what do you want in life? Do you have the answer on the tip of your tongue? If you do, congratulations—you are one of the 10 percent of all human beings who have taken the time to get clear on what you want out of life. If you don't know the answer to that question or want to know how to become even clearer, keep reading… I will provide you with a simple way to figure out what you do want and how to get really clear on it.

The habit of looking at and focusing on things you don't want attracts more of those things to you. Until you are able to leverage the things you don't enjoy to get clear on what you prefer, you will keep finding yourself getting stuck or moving slower than you really want to move.

We live in an inclusion-based universe. This means that the universe does not respond to our words…it responds to whatever we are giving our attention to and more importantly, how we are feeling about the focus of our attention. Have you ever noticed a repetitive pattern in your life that you don't enjoy, such as choosing boyfriends who are unfaithful or employers that are micromanagers or friends who treat you a way that you don't like? If you find yourself attracting repetitive situations that are unwanted, it is because usually you are so focused on what you don't want (to be cheated on, micromanaged, disrespected, taken advantage of, etc.) that you continue to attract it into your experience. You cannot give your attention to something, even if you're shouting no at it, without getting more of it and without the way you're feeling about it flowing to you.

The universe does not recognize the negative or positive, it only responds to what you are focused on. So when you use words and phrases like *no*, *stop*, and *I don't want that*, you are actually giving your attention to the thing that you don't want. The most common reason that people get "stuck" in life is because they are focused upon the things that they don't want to happen. So they keep getting more of it and because they don't understand why it keeps happening, they feel helpless to change their circumstances.

Fortunately, there is an easy way to know whether you are focused on something that is helping or hindering you. It is your own personal internal guidance system called your emotions. That's right, your emotions are your guide. When you feel negative emotions such as sadness, anger, jealousy, irritation, frustration, depression, or stress, it means that what you are focused on in that moment is not in alignment with the things that you want. And when you are feeling happy, optimistic, hopeful, loving, appreciative, excited, or passionate about something, it means in that moment, you are focused on thoughts that are moving you toward the life that you want. It really is that simple.

You see, when you are born, a part of you remains connected to all that is in a nonphysical energetic way. This is the soul part of you who knows your purpose and is guiding you toward everything that you want. This soul part of you supports every true desire that you want and has a much broader view of how it can come about. So your job is to line your thoughts up with the things that you want…to think thoughts that cause you to feel good and get excited about how fantastic your new position or boyfriend or car or whatever is going to be.

The moment you decide you want something different from what you have, your inner being agrees with and starts looking for ways to make it happen for you. The only things that slow the process are your observations of it not being there yet and your doubtful thoughts about how it probably won't happen, or trying to figure out how it will take place. It is not your job to figure out how to make things happen—that's the beauty of your inner being. It will figure out the how; your job in getting everything you want is to focus on why you want it and how it will feel when you have it, in an attitude of excited anticipation.

So the trick to turning unwanted things into positive things is this: when you find yourself focused on something you don't want, pause and ask yourself what it is. It helps to speak it out loud or write it down. For example: *I don't want to be in debt and I'm sick of not be able to afford the things I want.* Then ask yourself what is it that you *do* want, and state it in the positive: *I want to be wealthy; I want to feel abundant and free to be able to buy everything I want.* Or perhaps you've expressed this fear: *I'm worried about getting cancer; it's in my family, and it seems to be popping up everywhere. You never know who's going to get it and I have bad luck… I'll probably get it too.* What do you want? *I want to be healthy; I want to feel vibrant, youthful, and healthy all the days of my life.* Or maybe you've written this: *All the good men are taken. I always attract the jerks to me. I'm never going to find a partner who respects me, likes the same things*

I do, and sweeps me off my feet. Okay, so what do you want? *I want to find my dream partner. I want to attract a partner who loves me as much as I love him, who sweeps me off my feet and wants to work at creating our dream life together.*

Sometimes, when you're surrounded by situations that are not pleasing to you, it can be difficult to find a positive thought. The feeling that you are always searching for when you are deliberately trying to feel better is the feeling of relief. The best way to turn things around is to find something in your environment that you are grateful for. It could be that you've learned a lot, grown a lot, met someone who will link you to something that you seek, or simply that you're clearer on what you don't want...which in turn means that you're clearer on what you *do* want in this area.

Gratitude and appreciation are very powerful positive emotions that move you closer to all of your desires, along with joy, knowledge, freedom, love, empowerment, passion, enthusiasm, eagerness, happiness, belief, optimism, hopefulness, and contentment. If you make the effort to search for the silver lining in every situation and ignore the things that are bothering you as much as possible, your life experience has to change to match your new outlook and expectation level.

Here's one example of how quickly this tactic of turning your attention to what you want can work. A friend who found herself in a work situation that did not make her very happy emailed me this note:

I started working for this all-woman agency five months ago and it seemed so wonderful for the first month or so. After that, however, everyone's true colors revealed themselves, and it is by far the worst place that I have ever worked. I head into work with a stomachache almost every day because the women are so mean and so demeaning. For a long time I tried my hardest to be positive and to build a shell so the abusive atmosphere and negativity wouldn't affect me. But after trying for so long without any change, over the past two or three months, I have been desperately looking for a new place of employment. With the state of the economy, however, this has proven to be quite challenging.

Here's what happened to my friend within five days of doing the process I mentioned above:

OK, so you are not going to believe me when I tell you this... The day after I emailed you, a friend called me and said that there was an opening in her government office and that I should request a meeting with the director, as she'd recommended me for the position and the director was really keen to meet me. So I requested the meeting, and then for the rest of the week I really did exactly what you suggested to do, flipping my emotions around and focusing on the things I want. I met with the director last night and she offered me the job on the spot! It's twice the money that I'm making here and it's dealing with major, meaty issues and strategic communications, which is exactly what I wanted. I am going in to sign the contract tonight, and then I'm giving my two weeks' notice on Monday!!! Joanna!!! You were so right! It's just so unbelievable. In one hour (that was how long I met with the director) I managed to not only get my dream job, but twice as much pay and the security of working for the government! The universe is one phenomenal thing, I swear! Anyway, I wanted to thank you for keeping me focused with my eye on the prize. Now these next two weeks are going to fly by, and I will be so happy because I know there is a pot of gold at the end!

You see, life is supposed to be fun. It's supposed to be easier! The only "work" that you need to do is live your life and decide what you prefer, then align your thoughts and expectations with those things.

Life is meant to be playful and happy; you are supposed to feel good. You always get the things you are expecting to get, so make sure you're expecting really good stuff!

No one else knows better than you what is good for you. You don't need to live up to anyone else's standards. The sooner you start caring more about how you feel than what other people think of you or how they feel, the sooner you will speed up the pace of allowing what you want to come to you.

Realizing Your Personal Legend

"As the details of my Personal Legend continue to unfold, I am certain that every juncture along my life's path has critically contributed to my growth and the realization of my dream."

by E. L. Fitzgerald

E. L. Fitzgerald is a doctoral candidate at Boston University's School of Public Health. Upon graduation, she hopes to apply her military and nonprofit experience in leadership and management to improve the lives of women and children utilizing preventative measures and early intervention approaches. As a U.S. Coast Guard veteran and child advocate, she has accumulated a diversity of experience in over three dozen countries, all of which have guided her in the successful implementation of a multimillion-dollar children's initiative. She lives in Connecticut with her dog, Grace, and can be contacted at elf2103@columbia.edu.

Paulo Coelho in the *The Alchemist* wrote, "Your Personal Legend is what you have always wanted to accomplish. Everyone, when they are young, knows what their Personal Legend is. At that point in their lives, everything is clear and everything is possible. They are not afraid to dream, and to yearn for everything they would like to see happen to them in their lives."

My name is E. L. Fitzgerald. This chapter is about the realization of my Personal Legend, based on the support of a loving family and ceaseless encouragement from wonderful friends; faith in myself and the maximization of every opportunity afforded to me; and finally a dedication to fulfill an inner calling I have had for as long as I can remember. My passion to help improve the lives of our most vulnerable and disadvantaged has been my Personal Legend and the driver that has continued to push me forward despite the obstacles, challenges, and barriers that have arisen.

As a first-generation Filipina American, I had an appreciation early on that my life would be very different had I been born and raised in the Philippines. My upbringing contributed greatly to my strong desire to serve others, and my worldview was further shaped by being raised in a military family. My father's devotion to the United States Coast Guard introduced me to what would become a life of service and commitment. Hard work, determination, and reverence for my family and culture were values deeply instilled in me. These values, combined with an inner calling, have become the cornerstones motivating me to serve children.

I began my voyage on a purposeful mission at the United States Coast Guard Academy to not only study international relations as it relates to children, but also to gain leadership insight in one of the oldest humanitarian organizations in the country. Within the Coast Guard, both at the Academy and for the six years I served as a commissioned officer,

I was exposed to leadership and management experiences that continue to serve me well in my professional and personal development. My responsibilities and challenges grew exponentially, strengthened and supported by relationships that influenced my growth as an individual, a humanitarian, and a leader.

The faith and trust the Coast Guard placed in me as a young officer was the start of a significant period in my life. My first two tours of duty exposed me to international operations in nearly three dozen countries, where I managed more than 30 personnel and led teams on capacity-building missions in developing nations. Moreover, the Coast Guard provided me meaningful occasions to work on various community-based initiatives, including leading a 30-person multiagency effort to rebuild a school and community center in Cartagena, Colombia; volunteering at an orphanage in Ecuador; and refurbishing a children's home in Florida. In my experience working abroad, I witnessed firsthand the disparities and depravities that exist globally. This experience opened my eyes to the complexities of poverty and its disproportionate impact on children.

My final tour as the director of marketing allowed me to build an infrastructure and develop systems to support a nationwide marketing effort for the Coast Guard Academy. Additionally, I was provided opportunities to advocate for equal access to quality education for underrepresented youth. While my military experience was invaluable in building key leadership and team-building skills, my position did not fulfill my need to stay involved with children. Working with children has always provided me with a sense of balance and purpose. In an effort to stay connected with children on an individual and community level, I volunteered at an after-school program for low-income families in Florida, gave extra support to struggling fourth graders in an urban area of Virginia, worked with trauma-inflicted children living in a domestic abuse shelter, and acted as a big sister to a young girl in Connecticut who had lost her mother to AIDS and her father to the correctional system. Overall, the Coast Guard taught me much more than how to drive a boat, lead a crew, or manage resources. The organization taught me my first life lessons on how to identify individual strengths and areas of need and build a team from a group of individuals. With this as my foundation, I set out to fulfill my Personal Legend to serve children in a greater capacity.

Determined to further cultivate my skills, knowledge, and passion to serve children, I pursued my master's in international affairs at Columbia University's School of International Relations and Public Affairs (SIPA), during which time I interned and was hired to work with UNICEF on various children's issues. My experience with UNICEF highlighted for me the importance an integrated vision and approach has on an initiative's overall effectiveness. It also served as an awakening to my own need to work more closely on the community level in order to truly understand the issues unique to a particular culture or population. Furthermore, I yearned for the opportunity to utilize my leadership and management skills once again. My next position as the project director of an early childhood system of care allowed me to combine my experiences and skills from the Coast Guard and UNICEF to serve children and families within their communities.

As the project director of a $9.5 million federally funded early childhood initiative, I was responsible for the programmatic, administrative, and fiscal oversight of a community-based initiative known as Building Blocks. I was charged to lead a collaborative effort to develop and implement a comprehensive system of services and supports to meet the needs of families with young children facing social emotional challenges. I was amazed at how system-of-care values (being child-centered, family-driven, culturally competent, and community-based) resonated so deeply within me and truly embodied all that I had believed in since I began this journey.

Having the opportunity to lead and manage Building Blocks was a remarkable experience. The excitement of constructing the program from the ground up, including hiring a diverse staff, developing an infrastructure, and implementing an evidenced-based service delivery model, was both challenging and rewarding. Above all, I believe one of my most critical responsibilities as project director was to create a work environment conducive to nurturing the strengths and needs of each of my staff members so that as an effectively functioning team they could meet the individual and unique needs of the children and families we served. With nearly 20 staff members employed through five different community agencies co-located in one facility, one important challenge was to overcome cultural and historical divides. As our time together passed, the staff as a team became one of Building Blocks' greatest assets.

Building collaborative partnerships of families, providers, and community members across disciplines and cultures was another responsibility I gave high priority. By the end of our second year, I was leading and facilitating an early childhood collaborative with more than 40 members who shared an integrated vision to comprehensively address the needs of young children through the empowerment of families. Collaboration and community-based supports proved vital in meeting the needs of our children, 70 percent of whom were living at or below poverty level, 43 percent from single-mother homes, 49 percent having witnessed domestic violence, 50 percent living with someone with a mental illness including depression, 47 percent living with someone convicted of a crime, and about 42 percent living with someone with a substance abuse problem. After six months of providing free in-home services, we were able to prove a reduction in caregiver strain, maternal alcohol use, and child problem behaviors as well as an improvement in the child's ability to socialize with others, the child's competency level, and the child's ability to use self-control at six months of age. To my amazement, the realization of my Personal Legend was unfolding before my eyes.

My experience with Building Blocks, however, was not without its challenges. Changing systems and norms to support an integrated vision was, at times, limited by politics and system inefficiencies. As project director, I felt least prepared in my role to positively influence the political atmosphere. I faced the realization that not everyone embraces system-level change and that the larger community was not at a degree of readiness to undertake the work required to build an infrastructure and culture that supported a system that efficiently worked to meet the needs of the community's most needy children. One of the key leadership skills I recognized I needed to further develop was how to be an effective change agent for systems reform and how to remain passionate about what I believed in most but not allow my passion to blind me.

From Building Blocks, I transitioned to the director of performance improvement for a behavioral health and substance abuse agency serving adolescents and adults. I was responsible for assessing the adolescent programs and developing a comprehensive plan to improve quality of care. And although this position took me away from early intervention work, I learned that giving families the tools to succeed early on versus providing services as a bandage to deeply established issues was not only cost effective but also yielded more sustainable outcomes.

This chapter chronicles the realization of my Personal Legend to improve the lives of children. My next step toward this end is to complete my doctorate in maternal and child health. My desire to specialize in children's public health has manifested organically through my work and previous academic studies. With the experience of advocating for children from early childhood through adolescence, I have gained a comprehensive perspective on the compounding impact risk factors have over time, strengthening my conviction to focus on our youngest and most vulnerable children. I recognize the immense value early intervention and prevention efforts have in positively redirecting the trajectory of a child's life. I believe my leadership and management experience as a Coast Guard officer, coupled with my time at UNICEF and community nonprofits, has provided me with a solid foundation.

I hope to be part of the solution to systematically and

holistically address the issues that perpetuate poverty and disparity among our most disadvantaged children and families. As the details of my Personal Legend continue to unfold, I am certain that every juncture along my life's path has critically contributed to my growth and the realization of my dream.

Just One of the Guys

"With the great strides women have made over the last half-century, the world is really your oyster—but don't be surprised if you come across a little sand."

by Abby Goss

Abby Goss is a hydrologist with the U.S. Navy Facilities Engineering Service Center. She is a lieutenant commander in the U.S. Navy Reserves and currently resides in Ventura, California. She can be reached by email at abigail.d.goss@ gmail.com.

The opinions and views expressed in this article are those of the author only. They are not to be construed as official or representative of the U.S. Navy or any military service.

In the United States today, women comprise nearly half of the labor force, or approximately 46.5 percent. This is a significant increase from 50 years ago, when women made up about one-third of the workforce.

Over the last half-century, women have edged their way into essentially every civilian occupation imaginable, and are currently restricted from only a few remaining jobs in the military. So what can you expect if you choose to venture into one of these communities? While I write this chapter from a military perspective, it is really applicable to any woman out there who finds herself in a career field dominated by men. These career fields are often referred to as nontraditional occupations, and are designated as those occupations which are comprised of less than 25 percent women.

So, with the great strides women have made over the last half-century, the world is really your oyster—but don't be surprised if you come across a little sand.

Being a woman in a male-dominated world can be daunting and sometimes lonely. It is filled with professional, personal, and social challenges and, sometimes, pitfalls. You may feel afraid to offer your professional opinion because you are worried your colleagues won't take you seriously. You may feel ashamed to show emotion, whether that is anger, fright, or—oh, no!— tears, because they will think you are being a "girl." You may feel pressured to forgo family events, especially when it comes to children, because you are worried that your fellow employees will think you are requesting special "mom" time off. You may feel that you are not as professionally respected as your male counterparts, and be subjected to purposefully indiscreet discussions of affirmative action. And, being one of the few women in your field, you probably will have few female companions who can empathize. Even worse are those cases in which your female colleagues have become so ingrained in the male society that they acquiescently join in the behavior to dim the spotlight on them or to gain added acceptance by co-workers.

Since graduating from high school in 1992, I have

worked almost consistently in a male-dominated world. I attended the U.S. Naval Academy, which had about 12 percent women in my year group. That was one of my first glimpses into the world of testosterone I was about to enter. When I reported to my first ship in 1998, it had only recently been converted to accommodate women, and I checked in as the second woman attached to this ship. There were just three female officers on board among a crew of about 380 men as we made the trek across the Pacific from Japan to Washington State, where we finally took on more female sailors.

Eighteen months later, I left my ship to enter the training program for an even more male-dominated society—the nuclear Navy. In this specialty, sailors are trained to operate the nuclear reactors for submarines and aircraft carriers. Female engineers are hard to come by in the nuclear community, and they are not always welcomed. Within the first few days of checking on board the aircraft carrier, I had a pleasant conversation with one of the leading enlisted men in my division. It ran something like this:

"Ma'am, don't worry about coming down into the engineering spaces. You can just stay up here in the office."

"Excuse me?"

"We got it. Don't worry about it. You aren't needed down there."

"What if I need to sign something for verification?"

"We'll bring the paperwork up to you."

"That's my signature and my butt on the line. I don't think so..."

In 2002, I left active duty to pursue other interests, but stayed affiliated with the military as a Reservist. In 2007, I deployed to the Horn of Africa in support of the Global War on Terror. I found myself on a base of approximately 1,500 military, about 150 of whom were women. As the project manger for humanitarian water projects, I was one of the few military who regularly traveled to several African countries to coordinate water projects and workshops. There I was, a relatively young female (early 30s), representing the military and the engineers, liaising with African partners, directing the activities of various engineering units (90 percent of which are male), while trying to broach social, cultural, and religious divides. It sometimes took a little while for Muslim village elders to accept that the person they had to deal with was not only the youngest-looking person in the group, but also a woman.

Based on these varied experiences, I have tried to determine what sort of guidance I can give to ambitious, intelligent young women who may find themselves on the brink of such adventures themselves. I have come up with a list of guidelines that I have imparted to other women throughout the years. They were often responses to lamentations about their jobs, their situations, or the military, but can really be applied to any woman who struggles to establish herself in a community dominated by men. So here it goes:

1. **Perception is everything!** Because there were few women where I worked, it was not unusual for me to eventually find a good male friend with whom I felt comfortable. We would chat or have a drink or meals together, as female friends normally would, but inevitably

the rumors would surface within a short amount of time that we were seeing one another. Unfairly, it does not matter whether the situation or scenario really is as it may seem. You will never be able to fight the rumors. If you are not willing to tolerate them, don't put yourself in that situation. Only perception, not reality, matters when it comes to your reputation.

2. **Acknowledge the double standard.** Everyone has heard, and has probably even witnessed, this double standard: If a guy sleeps with a lot of girls, he is a stud. If a girl sleeps with a lot of guys, she is a [*fill in your descriptor of choice*]. This is especially true in a male-dominated community. For example, you will often hear people say that the woman was promoted because of her gender or looks, whereas a man is *always* promoted because of his qualifications (right, as if the "old-boys club" never happens!). These situations and insults will inevitably occur at some point to you or someone you know. Though you don't have to accept it, it is certainly something of which you should be cognizant.

3. **Get used to the glass house.** This guideline goes hand-in-hand with the previous two. Working in a male-dominated community is good practice for politics, because you can guarantee that your actions will be subtly watched and discussed even if they are not, in your opinion, worthy of discussion. A short time ago, I was approached by a young man while I was in Newport, Rhode Island, who asked me if I had recently deployed to Africa. I could have sworn I had never seen this person before in my life, and yet he was able to recognize me 18 months later as I stepped out of a random building

on a base 8,000 miles away from where he first saw me. Accept the fact that you stand out, that you are a novelty in the workplace. People will be watching your moves and your actions, whether you realize it or not. And men gossip just as much as women…

4. **Fight the urge to grow a (big) pair.** There is a tendency for women to feel as though they need to become one of the guys in order to be accepted by them. There is no need to give up your femininity. Believe it or not, the men like the diversity you add to the group. One of the most frequent comments I would hear around my first ship was that we were like "a breath of fresh air." Men may feel that you bring color, rejuvenation, energy, and youth to the workplace. So wear that fabulous scarf if you want. And don't be afraid to venture beyond the drab gray and black. However, though it's great to express your femininity, it is also wise to temper it with moderation. As in any profession, you want your appearance to say "professional, confident, sophisticated." When you leave the room, you want your colleagues to comment on your competence, not your strong perfume.

Inevitably, though, you will probably find yourself mirroring the men in your workplace in some fashion. One of the most common ways that I see this is through language—more specifically, through foul language. It is a phenomenon that we in the Navy call a "sailor's mouth." This is when nearly every sentence you utter has a four-letter word in it, the most frequent of which is the f-bomb. In the military, I can walk from office to office and never be fazed by any colorful language I may hear, but as soon as I am off base and I hear a 20-year-old in the coffee shop drop an f-bomb, I'm surprised. I can't explain it; I just know that I notice it. And if I notice it, you can be sure that other people who aren't so accustomed to it are also taken aback. So, while it is not a problem to use it in the workplace if your co-workers are okay with it (I use it rather frequently in certain situations), I caution against making it a habit because it is hard to stop when you are again in public or among mixed company.

5. **Know the difference between earning versus deserving respect.** This is a topic that is near and dear to me as a military member—not because I am an officer and frequently have subordinates assigned to me, but because I see it so often abused not just in the military but in the civilian world as well. When supervisors feel they are losing control of a situation, some (both male and female) will get defensive and demand respect from subordinates because of their position. As a female supervisor in a male-dominated community, you will most likely at some point feel you do not receive the same level of consideration given by subordinates to your male colleagues. My case in point is the conversation I related earlier—I can guarantee that conversation never would have occurred if I were male. The best thing you can do in these situations is to acknowledge the person's opinion and do your job. My response was, "I understand you feel like you don't need me down in the engineering spaces, but I would be a poor supervisor if I had no idea what was going on down there. Not to mention, it is illegal for me to sign forms without checking on the status personally." Twelve months later, this same petty officer came to me before transferring off the ship and

thanked me for coming down to the engineering spaces every day. He said it meant a lot to the junior personnel to know that I cared enough about them and their work to be down there with them.

I hope that these brief tips will give you some insight into what you can expect as you enter a world in which women are in the minority. Don't let this chapter daunt or dissuade you—we need more women in these communities! By accepting and adapting to some of the challenges of this unique world, you can succeed in a career field that can be very rewarding and fulfilling.

Discovering Your Path

"If you love what you do, you will succeed."
by Amber P. Buck

Amber Buck is currently the Learning and People Development manager for Frank, Rimerman & Co. LLP, the largest locally owned public accounting firm in California. Her academic background—a master of arts degree in Leadership Studies from the University of San Diego and a bachelor of science in Accounting from San Jose State University—has prepared her well for this role. Every day she delicately balances ways to meet the needs of the hearts and intellectual minds within her organization.

Amber works with the University of San Diego's Leadership for Change Conferences and was selected to participate in the Leadership Institute for the California Society of CPAs. In her free time, Amber enjoys exercise (particularly spinning, running, and Bikram yoga), cooking healthy, delicious foods, and eating dark chocolate. She resides in San Diego, California with her fiancé, Todd, and a spunky Pomeranian named Leroi.

I was a "surprise" to my parents. They went on one date and on that night I was conceived. When I was born, my father was a 35-year-old high school teacher. My mother was 19 and recently graduated from the school where my father taught. They got married, I guess, because of me.

It shouldn't come as a surprise that their marriage was short-lived. My mother left the house when I was 10 months old. What surprises people most about my story is the fact that my mother didn't raise me; my father did. It took my own experience of being a teenager to understand why my mother left us. Can you imagine what it would be like to be a child, pregnant with your own child, *and* married to an old man you barely knew? No thank you!

Although she had visitation rights, my mom was never really in my life growing up. She chose to spend her time nurturing a drug habit instead of me. When I did see her, the visit was usually traumatic and entailed my being exposed to things children shouldn't see, such as drugs, lies, and crime.

My father was an okay dad for about the first five years. Today we don't speak, because his alcoholism has driven a wedge between us. Over the years, I don't know whether his actions worsened as time went on or I became more aware of right versus wrong. I remember him being pulled over for drunk driving and both of us being hauled into the police station. I remember what weekends were like when he didn't have a hangover (activity filled) versus when he did (sedentary). I remember moving in with friends twice during high school because home life felt so unstable. I also recall how the dynamics shifted when he invited his girlfriend to live with us.

Like my mother, my dad's girlfriend had a drug

problem. Growing up in a house with an alcoholic and a drug addict, while longing to see a mother who only exposed me to worse environments, was unhealthy to say the least.

So what does my family history have to do with finding your vocational path? I share my history because I feel too many people use the absence of kind, nurturing parents as an excuse for why they cannot achieve what they want from life. I didn't have anyone sit down and do homework with me. I didn't have anyone to encourage me to go to college. *Your experiences are all a matter of perspective.* The way I see my story, I did have role models. The parental figures in my life did a great job of modeling behavior I never want to exhibit. I grew up knowing exactly who I didn't want to be.

Immediately after high school graduation, I moved out of the house and away to school. I needed to escape the madness. I didn't have my shit together entirely—in fact, I was far from having it together—so I couldn't go directly into a four-year degree program. Rather, I moved in with my grandparents to go to a community college. (Note: If you've grown up without good caretakers, find others to fill the gaps. My grandparents filled some voids and were instrumental in my healthy development.) It took me almost four years—twice as long as is standard—to graduate. In my defense, I took off one year to live abroad. I strongly encourage people to live overseas for at least six straight months. Anyone who has done so will tell you the experience is eye-opening and transformational. The other reason it took me so long to get through community college was that I had to learn a bunch of stuff I should have learned in high school: effective study habits, taking specific courses to meet requirements, and time management, as well as the fact that schoolwork is more important than boys and parties.

As I neared the end of my community college career and got ready to transfer to a four-year institution, I knew I had to choose a major. Someone gave me the idea of business marketing, which I was all set to select until I enrolled in a mandatory course on that path—accounting.

The study of accounting seems to be either a love or hate experience for most people. And I loved it! Most people struggled in the class, while I aced the exams with minimal effort. The stuff just made sense to me, so I began to inquire about careers in accounting. I learned all the things I wanted to hear: I could make good money, which was important after an upbringing without luxuries; there would be many job opportunities upon graduation; and the position offered something I longed for—respect for my intellect. I hate to come off as conceited, but, in this society, I am perceived as pretty. Also in this society, and perhaps others, pretty doesn't equate to intelligent. In fact, people usually expect pretty girls to be dumb, naïve, and/or not very ambitious. My decision to become an accountant was extremely empowering.

I vividly recall being in an upper-division business course that was required for all business majors. It was just after I'd completed my first professional position as a summer intern with Ernst and Young. I sat in class, minding my business, with my EY notepad. The student next to me, whom I had never spoken with before, struck up a conversation with me. "EY," he began, "I didn't know they had marketing internships." I could not believe this guy wrongly assumed I wasn't intelligent enough to (gasp!) actually have earned myself a coveted position as an accounting intern and was responsible and intelligent enough to work on audits of publicly traded companies. It felt *so* good to tell him his assumption was wrong and show him that pretty girls could take a seat in the boardroom.

As I continued to share my career path with others, for the first time, people seemed to immediately respect me. I began to accept that I didn't meet people's expectations and even learned how to graciously respond to a phrase I heard all too often: "You don't look like an accountant."

As I forged my path, I found a great company to work for upon graduation. I chose to work in their tax department, and boy did I work. The hours were long and hard. The work felt grueling. During the busy season, as the deadline for filing taxes approached, I remember waking up every day and counting down the days until it was over. "Only a few more days left," I'd have to tell myself just to make it out of bed.

With the exception of the great people I worked with, everything about the job felt like hell. I hated the hours. I hated the work. I hated the prospect of a lifetime of vacations planned around deadlines established by the government. For the first time in awhile, I didn't want to be an accountant and I had *no* idea what I wanted to be.

I realized I was headed down the wrong path and needed to find a new one. If I didn't look like an accountant, what did I look like? To get that answer, I had to figuratively look in a mirror and find some self-reflection.

If you ever find yourself in this situation, on the wrong path and hating the work that you do, ask yourself the following:

- What would get me excited to get up out of bed every day?
- Do I want to talk to people all day, some of the day, or never?
- What projects/tasks do I enjoy?
- Do I prefer to sit in an office or do I need to be out and about?
- What types of people do I enjoy?
- Do I like continuously learning new skills or do I want to learn some fundamental principles and be done?

After you have come up with answers to these questions, your path may emerge. It did for me. When I thought through these questions, I came to realize I loved to attend all the university recruiting events which my company asked me to represent them. I loved to talk with the students. I loved to travel to the different campuses. I loved to coordinate events and help students transition from academia to the world of business.

Also, don't just rely on yourself if you are in this quandary. Ask others what they think of you as a dentist, a veterinarian, a court reporter, a personal trainer, a boutique owner, a postal carrier, an author, a photographer, an acupuncturist, a whatever it is you want to become. No one ever saw me as an accountant, but I didn't want to hear it. I should have listened.

In some instances, you might also consider going back to school. (And yes, I know school might not be for everyone but it sure does make you more marketable, and no matter how smart you are, you can learn a whole lot more.) I decided to pursue a master's degree. When searching for schools, my number-one criterion was that the curriculum not be numbers-based, because I did not want to crunch one more number. I found an amazing program that allowed me to take electives in any discipline I chose. My master's gave me a better understanding of myself and helped me to better see what I can contribute to this world. As with accounting, I excelled in my courses. I earned a 3.94 GPA, and in accounting it was only a 3.22. Okay, so the accountant in me is clearly not entirely dead and I still like numbers a little. But seriously, I believe these numbers display clear evidence that you will excel if you are doing what you love. I always tell the students I work with to follow their hearts. If you love what you do, you will succeed.

Today, I still work for the same accounting firm where I started my career right after my undergraduate degree. However, today, my role is entirely different. Half of my job is in university recruiting, which entails finding students to work for our firm and preparing them and the company for their first year. The other half is centered on learning and development. Anything that has to do with training and the development of our professionals crosses my desk. I love my job! I have never had to count down the days until a project was over. And, for the record, all of my job duties require what accounting required of me—a whole lot of brainpower.

A Not-So-Linear Path

"When I counsel others in the area of career development,
I ask them to define their vision and goal."
by Julianna Hynes, PhD

Julianna is a gifted leadership development consultant, coach, and facilitator as well as a talented author and speaker. With more than 10 years of education and experience in human resources, training, and coaching, she honed those talents to become the founder and CEO of Julianna Hynes & Associates (JHA)—a leadership development firm specializing in and assisting emerging women leaders and the organizations that employ them in identifying, bridging, and achieving career and organizational goals. In addition to her entrepreneurial activities, Julianna serves as an online faculty member for the University of Phoenix, teaching various topics in psychology. She holds a bachelor's degree in Psychology, a master's degree in Organizational Consulting, and a PhD in Organizational Psychology, in which she studied the career development and success strategies of professional, high-status African American women.

Julianna is a passionate and energetic leadership development professional who motivates, encourages, and inspires her clients to achieve sustainable, life-changing breakthroughs and over-the-top results. For speaking, coaching, and consulting engagements, seminars, and book orders or signing engagements, Julianna can be reached at www.xlence. org.

Growing up as an African American girl in the San Francisco Bay Area during the 1970s and '80s was very much a blessing. I was raised by both my parents in the suburbs, and they worked hard at providing a comfortable life for us. I went to a racially diverse school and had friends of many different cultures. I grew up happy and without a care in the world. Preparing for school one day, I remember standing in the bathroom, looking at myself in the mirror and talking with my mother as she brushed my hair. We were having one of our many conversations about what I wanted to be when I grew up. I always aspired to be a professional, and my mother and I enjoyed talking about my career choices and options. While very supportive, my mom cautioned me that because I was African American and female, when I entered the workforce, I would have to work twice as hard to be considered only half as good. I didn't understand it at the time but in hindsight, I realize my mother was preparing me for what she thought was the inevitable. As I continued to gaze at my image in the mirror, I started to wonder how such a small thing as being female and black would hinder me from achieving my dreams. Because of my upbringing in a racially mixed environment, I had no early notion of racial or gender inequality. That early-morning conversation with my mother was the beginning of what would be a lifelong learning experience.

As I got older, I slowly began to experience what my

other had shared years ago. My first lesson in being treated differently happened in high school when I was 16 or 17 years old. When I shared with my school guidance counselor my goal of becoming a doctor, she recommended that I set my sights on a community college rather than the university I told her I wanted to attend. Her rationale? A community college would be easier for me to get into and I could learn a trade in case medical school didn't work out. She influenced me enough to adjust my plan and settle on applying to a college that was not as academically challenging as my target school.

I decided to study psychology even though I was a pre-med major and for two years, although socially I had a good time (a *really* good time), intellectually, something was missing; I was bored. Before my second year was over, at the age of 19, I decided to apply to my first-choice school just to see if I would get in and, guess what, I did! After I received the news, I made plans to transfer my junior year of college—continuing to major in psychology and taking all of my science courses in order to apply to medical school after I got my undergrad degree. Two years later, right before my 22nd birthday, I received my bachelor of science degree in Psychology from the University of California.

Now, one can only speculate why my high school counselor recommended a junior college for me. It might have had nothing to do with my race or gender, and I'm not holding any grudges against her. Trust me! I actually look back at that situation and see what the lessons were. I learned that I can accept feedback but do not necessarily have to follow someone else's suggestion. I learned to listen to my spirit and that inner voice that tells me what to do. I learned that it is okay to seek guidance and speak with those who have wisdom, but age doesn't always equate to good judgment. As a child, I was taught to respect my elders and I did, but I also learned that respecting them and *always* following their advice did not represent good judgment on my part. God did give me a mind of my own to use. As I have gotten older, I have also learned to pray first and then seek out wisdom if I am still in need of direction.

After graduating from college, at the age of 22, I decided to get married (something I didn't pray about first). A year later, the marriage was over, I was pregnant, and instead of going to medical school as I had planned, I decided to enter the workforce after my baby was born.

Since I was temporarily (or so I thought) taken off course from achieving my dream to be a doctor and I didn't have a backup plan, I pursued a job that would fit my skill set and pay the most. I found a position as an administrative assistant in a male-dominated organization. At first, I was content, as it paid well enough and I didn't have to worry about working nights or weekends—that way, I could be with my son. About a year after getting hired, however, I learned that I was making less money than my peers because of my job level, regardless of having a degree. As a result, I began expressing an interest in advancing beyond my administrative role into a more professional, managerial position, but as I made efforts to pursue this new goal (such as going back and getting a master's degree), I experienced challenges that my male counterparts did not. These challenges were a lack of acknowledgment or support of my professional goals, lack of opportunities to discuss or even be considered for advancement opportunities, and even at one point being discouraged from applying to positions that would afford me a higher salary, more responsibility, and more mobility in the organization.

Whether it was because of my status as a single mother or my administrative role, opportunities in this organization did not abound; I quickly learned that my intelligence, hard work, and even my educational attainments were not sufficient for me to transition into a managerial position. Despite having a master's degree and receiving outstanding performance reviews, I was not advancing and I did not know, nor was I told, why. Although those posing the challenges were not overt in their opposition, I couldn't help wonder whether my inability to advance was because I was black, female, or both. My mother's advice slowly came back to me, and I discovered, by speaking with other African American women, that my experience was not unique.

I decided to leave that organization when I was 31, after six years of hard work, and moved on to a company that was better at nurturing the careers of their diverse workforce. There, I learned, grew, and positioned myself to start my own business two years later, at age 33. Since then I have earned my doctorate degree (fulfilling the dream of being a doctor, just not a medical doctor), I have established a successful coaching and consulting practice, and I have the opportunity to meet many women who are aspiring to go beyond the glass ceiling to achieve their professional goals.

Now, at 40, looking back on my young adult and early career experiences, I can see what I didn't know but organically learned along the way. First, I didn't know about finding and having mentors, both within and outside of the organization. You see, while my mother and other women in my family were wonderful examples, only one individual talked with me as an adult about my professional choices and work ethic. Although I formed relationships within the organization, I did not know how to strategically identify those who could guide me through the organizational politics and challenges that I faced.

Second, I didn't know that it was important to be in a position that allowed for a lot of exposure to other aspects of the organization. Although as an administrative assistant I learned quite a bit working for one of the managers, I wasn't included in decision-making discussions and had not developed the business acumen to be able to successfully participate in those discussions even if I was included. I was deficient in areas that I didn't know would help my career, and I didn't know that these deficiencies affected how people perceived me as a professional.

Third, I didn't know that flexibility and consistency were key. By flexibility, I mean being willing to move from one organization to another in order to obtain the knowledge and skill sets I was looking to acquire. I was expecting one company to meet my professional needs and groom me, rather than strategically plotting my course. By consistency, I mean not only being consistent in my work habits and ethic, but also in my demeanor and interactions with others. As a single parent, I was finding it difficult to balance my role as a mom with my desire to develop my career. Unknowingly to me early on, the two clashed and both were affected by the other. It took a couple of years to figure that out.

Finally, I didn't know the importance of networking

and developing relationships throughout the organization and beyond. While I did all of these things organically, for me, what was missing was a clear career development plan. Now, when I counsel others in the area of career development, I ask them to define their vision and goal. I ask them what things they are planning to do to accomplish their goal, and what other people they need to include in this plan, because we never go it alone. Some parts of your career will unfold as you execute your plan, while there will also be surprises along the way. Be flexible, be focused, and be persistent. Enjoy the process, enjoy your life, and enjoy the ride.

Mommy, Be Nice

"Just like our children, we have to learn and mature, understand our surroundings, and decide how we best navigate."

by Corina Dubois

Corina Dubois is a communications and marketing consultant. Once heralded as a rising star in political arenas, Corina shifted the focus of her consultancy to reflect that of her toughest job—raising three boys, being a military wife, and navigating the mom market. She founded Celebrate Mama! LLC, an award-winning national event series and online resource focused on moms who are business owners themselves. The Celebrate Mama! event series weaves together the best resources a community has to offer mothers. The brand, planning tools, and Web affiliation are available as a license, allowing other entrepreneurial women to create unique events, support other local businesses, and give back to their communities all at the same time. Corina acts as the managing CEO of Celebrate Mama!, mentoring other license holders, entrepreneurs, and women seeking a credible platform to launch their businesses ideas. She has a Communications/Political Science degree from the University of Maryland, is a decorated U.S. Navy Veteran, and is an active member of professional development and educational organizations. Corina is currently attending The George Washington University's Political Management Program, and works from her home office in San Diego, California. Learn at www.celebratemama.com

Remember that girl in middle school who smirked at what you were wearing? She'd catch your eye in the lunchroom and in one glance, make you embarrassed at how many Tater Tots you just ate? Or, you could tell she'd overheard the tail end of your conversation and you spent the rest of the day replaying in your head how you sounded? I remember her, and even though I'm older now and can look back and realize she was probably insecure, or overcompensating for someone who wasn't nice to her, I'm still relieved to have grown out of that pressure-filled stage of life.

How come I found that girl again, but this time in my Mommy & Me playgroup? How come I saw her at my stroller fitness class? How come she's there next to me at the preschool drop-off, and then online at all the websites I visit? Is it because there are still mean girls out there, 15 years later, or is it because we all are unaccustomed to the pressures of being a mom? In all honesty, it's some of both, and many moms just aren't nice.

I quickly absorbed—as a new mom—that this pressure went farther than teenage fashion. It wasn't about my diaper bag or the type of stroller I had. It was deeper than that. It was about me. As a woman. As a mom. As a person who is new to something and faced with decisions that are life-altering and emotional and charged and defining all at once. I was being judged for being me, and I couldn't understand why this was happening. I wondered: Why am

I learning this now, when there is so much else going on? Why hadn't any other mom-friends told me there would be this pressure to be perfect? Why was no one communicating anything other than judgment?

Moms are, in effect, functioning at the same stage as their children, regardless of their years as a woman on this planet. Meet a pregnant mom and she is brimming with the hope of what is happening in her life; she is developing in her new role. Meet a brand-new mother and she is excited, confused, and unable to take it all in at once, trying to figure out how things work, just like her infant who still yearns for the comfort of the small and familiar. Meet a mom of a preschooler and she, too, is stretching her legs, learning at record speed, trying to keep up with what's so overwhelmingly in front of her. It goes on…the mom with school-aged kids who has to be focused on the logistics of a schedule, meeting expectations set by schools, sports, peers, hormones… It does not matter if these moms are 25 or 35, they are all immediately reduced to a perspective that mirrors the age of their children, because they are thrust wholly into their own new being as a mother.

Just like our children, we have to learn and mature, understand our surroundings, and decide how we best navigate. But women don't communicate how to do this. Instead, we expect, with lines drawn in the sand, E-X-P-E-C-T other women to naturally "get it." And we judge people who don't. And then we ostracize them. Talk about pressure. Talk about not playing nice!

When my oldest son was about a year and a half, there was a mom-and-daughter team in our playgroup. The little girl used to hit my son in the face with puzzle pieces. The mom would avoid the situation, and every week we would go to this playgroup, and every week they would be at the puzzle table, and every week this girl would hit my son, and every week I would say, "We don't hit, little girl," and every week I would look over at the mom and shake my head in disdain that she was not paying attention. Not one of those weeks did I go over and talk with the mom about it. Instead, we left the playgroup. I just expected that mom to know this was not the right behavior. I expected her to get a handle on her daughter. I expected that my son be treated better. I expected to know a better way to handle this, but I didn't, so we left. I was 29 at the time, and I had no idea how to outthink a one-year-old.

So, a couple of months after we had been attending the playgroup, we were at an event—my own event for moms and kids—and here comes this mom with her puzzle-wielding daughter. She walked right up to me and told me she missed us. Told me she was looking for a job and wondered if I was hiring. Told me she wanted to be with her daughter and work at the same time. She told me they had been having challenges with behavior and were trying to be around as many positive influences as possible. She told me all of this just as quickly as I told it to you, as if she had been going over it in her head wondering how it would sound.

I was dumbfounded.

Here I had been all uppity about my own expectations, none of which I actually articulated to someone over 18 months old, but I really was the one letting people down. I was not sharing in motherhood with this mom. I was the one staring and trying to make her feel shame for this puzzle thing. I thought I was being nice, but in reality I didn't communicate at all with her. I blocked her. I ran from her. And, I taught my son to do the same thing. I taught her daughter that this is how she should be treated, all because she didn't know how to handle herself at the puzzle table.

Whoa.

No, I did not hire her. That *would* make a nice story, but I didn't need the help and I still didn't want to open myself up professionally to these challenges. But I did rejoin the playgroup. And her daughter *did* hit my son in the face with a puzzle piece again.

But this time, I talked with the mom.

"Excuse me, you may not have seen that Amber hit Holden in the face just now."

"Oh, yeah, she always does that. I've tried to tell her. I don't know what to do anymore."

"Maybe we could tell her together."

Maybe we should talk about our expectations, share in some strategies, and work on this together since none of us know what to do on our own. I don't want to be the bad mom, either, you know.

We went back over to the kids and I had Holden tell this girl she'd hurt him in the face with the puzzle piece. It would *also* be a nice story to relate to you how they shook hands and it never happened again. They really just stared at each other.

And it did happen again after that. But from then on, we could talk openly about our expectations. I didn't have to run from this playgroup or this mom or my own feelings of superiority or expectations—or my fear of not getting it right myself. The pressure was gone because we communicated openly.

I didn't know I had to say, "Hey, tell your kid to stop hitting with puzzle pieces." But I did. Because really what I was saying was, "Hey, you are important enough in this relationship that we should all get along at the puzzle table. Let's all learn from this."

We're not born with this stuff. We have to learn it; preferably, together. In doing so, I was no longer the middle-school girl in the cafeteria, hoping to shame someone into self-awareness and change.

In truth, we're all faced with the puzzles at the table, not really knowing what to do when someone isn't nice. Or when someone doesn't meet our expectations. Or when someone doesn't see we're really all learning this at the same rate. Or when we don't know what to do or how to be a big girl about it. That's why as women, we have to communicate about motherhood and share what we're learning, instead of expecting others to just know it. That girl—well, a figurative representation of her—is now in my son's first-grade classroom. We are going to have to deal with her and her mom in one capacity or another. I'd much rather it be about puzzle pieces in the face and not scratches to the groin, as in a new situation we are facing with another kid.

But, I digress.

Most of us teach our children by setting an example, explaining how things work, and acting patiently in the understanding that we are on a journey. Seeing the light bulbs go off in our kiddos and the connections made is part of the fun of being a mom! So, if we know other moms are at that same level, then it makes sense that we would give each other these same lessons, the same patience, the same tools, and the same communication.

The flip side to all this is that there are those women who don't care to be nice. And no amount of froufrou let's-get-along is going to change that. As a business owner who has focused solely on the "mom market" for the past six years, I have seen thousands of moms interact with one another, and I have dealt with my fair share of straight-up jealousy, maliciousness, gossip, and outright selfishness.

I have stayed awake at night, replaying conversations that were taken out of context. I have allowed my business to suffer in order to try and mentor other women who are new moms and new in business. I have lost friendships over business decisions that I made trying to keep everyone happy. I have cried with my kids about not understanding how things work or how I can make them better. And I have grown up from that. I'm six now, like my oldest son.

Now, I can say—as a mom who has had a chance to figure out who I am in these roles—that I have asked moms to talk *with* me and not *about* me. I have fired moms for not doing their jobs, and I have flat-out kept my distance from some moms who require way more energy than I can give. I have set my own boundaries and have drawn new lines of expectations, ones that revolve around being nice, being supportive, and being open in communication. Mean girls need not apply.

This chapter isn't about why it takes a village to raise kids and loving everyone we meet because she has changed diapers in the middle of the night. It's about opening the lines of communication with those women whom we choose to support. It's about growing up with the pace of our children and mirroring the principles we instill in them. It's about teaching our kids to be nice to others, and also about teaching ourselves to be nice to women who are growing up as "mom."

We wouldn't stand at the puzzle table letting our kid get hit in the face over and over again. We wouldn't take our kid to a middle-school cafeteria to be laughed at for what she ate or what she wore. But our reactions to this can teach our children about what it really means to be nice. We have to set aside the expectation for moms to get it all at once; we have to choose to take away this pressure and replace it with open communication.

I want us all to figure out how this puzzle fits together (preferably without getting hit in the nose with a pre-fab cardboard cutout). I want us to share in what we are learning through the stages of childhood. I want us all to grow up with our kids and enjoy this journey. It's the only time we're thrust into a whole new world, a whole new set of rules and rights and wrongs and expectations. It's the only time we have with our kids to teach them about how to be graceful under pressure. I want us all to be nice, mommy.

Life Happens Despite the Plan and the Doubters

"I was able to not postpone life to accord with my plan, my life goals were achieved much earlier than I thought possible."

By Janice H. Kurth, MD, PhD

Janice Kurth earned her bachelor's degree from Austin College, her PhD in human genetics at Stanford University, and her MD from the University of Arizona, with postgraduate training in internal medicine. Her professional career has included academic and industrial biomedical research, product development, research management, and pharmaceutical medicine. She is currently an independent consultant for biomedical and pharmaceutical companies. Janice lives in California with her husband of 23 years. She has two college-age daughters. Janice is active in several community organizations, including Rotary International. She may be contacted at jkurth1@san.rr.com.

My love of science began on a very specific day in the seventh grade, and the path of my life was set in motion. In my life sciences class, I observed an onion root tip under a microscope, and I could see with my own eyes real chromosomes and cells dividing. I was hooked. It was at this time that I instantaneously began to formulate a long-term plan for my future. I would grow up and be a scientist, and nothing would get in my way!

My life progressed through the remainder of my youth according to this plan. I took all the advanced science classes I could at my high school, worked in university laboratories every summer, entered the science fairs, was named the "Outstanding Science Student" my senior year, and applied to college to study science. The "master plan" was progressing as intended. Upon entering college, I began a premedical training program, as I was uncertain whether medical school or graduate school (to obtain a PhD) would be my path. I studied hard in college, received good grades, continued to work in hospital and/or laboratory settings during my summers, completed a College Honors thesis, and took pre-admission tests for both medical and graduate school. When it was time to apply to graduate school, I could not decide between pursuing an MD or a PhD, so I decided to do both! This was when my "master plan" became etched in stone. I was accepted into a National Institutes of Health fully funded MD/PhD program. My life was set for the next seven to nine years. No man, woman, or child would interfere. I, along with my parents, purchased a condo near my university. I moved in, started classes three days after my college graduation, and the ball was rolling.

Very soon thereafter, real life started to encroach on my perfectly planned life. After being in graduate school just over a year, an acquaintance that I had known for about 18 months, since the time that I'd applied to my graduate program, stopped me in the hall and told me that he "*needed*" to tell me something. Not "wanted," "desired," or anything else—"needed." I couldn't imagine why this person would need to tell me anything in particular. He proceeded to tell me how he was going to be going halfway across the country to do a residency program 15 months from now. I congratulated him. As I walked away, I was puzzled as to why this was important information for him to impart to me. I soon learned why.

This man and I started dating shortly after that puzzling hallway encounter and we quickly fell in love. Every whistle and bell in my head and heart began to go off. While I knew from a very early age that marriage and family was something that was important to me and that I desired this as part of my life, I certainly did not want it now! My life was "set" until I finished my graduate program and had launched my career, and nothing could get in the way of that. Marriage was something that would happen at some distant point in my future! However, I knew in my heart that this was the man I wanted to spend the rest of my life with. He was planning to move far away in a year. What was a young woman to do? My plan was being disrupted!

After much soul searching and many discussions with my very loving, caring, loyal husband-to-be, we came up with a new plan. I could apply to do the PhD portion of my degree program where he was doing his residency. I would take a leave of absence from my current institution and could return there to finish my MD when he was finished with his residency and I with my PhD. Because of my hard work in college, I had no problem getting accepted into the PhD program that I desired. There was one complicating factor, however. I was *not* going to uproot my education and move across country without a firm commitment from this man and a ring on my finger! Therefore, we became engaged and planned to be married a few weeks before the scheduled move. "Okay," I said to myself, "this isn't *the* plan, but it is an alternate plan that can work." For the first time in my life, I was able to compromise and adapt on a life-course issue. I was certain that I did not want to give up having this man in my life because of my stubborn plans. I was able to see that my multiple desires did not need to be mutually exclusive.

The revised plan was put in place, and then it was time to speak to our parents. I had a bit of anxiety regarding this. I was not an atypical daughter in that I probably spent my first 18 years motivated almost exclusively by the approval and pride of my parents. There was no greater reward for me than hearing "We are proud of you." I did not know what to expect as I announced this change in my life plan to my parents, especially my father. Matt, my husband-to-be, took the traditional route and asked my father for permission to marry me. My father insensitively replied with a request that I be allowed to achieve at least one of my doctorate degrees. Matt was flabbergasted! His goal was to do everything in his power to help me achieve both degrees I desired and he could not believe that my father showed such little confidence in us. I was cut to the core upon hearing this response, which further increased my resolve to achieve my goal just to show him and the rest of the world that I could!

Soon another major disruption in my perfect plan reared its head. As Matt and I were planning for our life together, we both knew that we wanted children. During such a discussion, Matt said, "I don't want to be 50 when I have children." Now, I can do simple math. Given that he was already 32, eight years my senior, and I had a good nine to ten years of education ahead of me, I concluded that children, too, would not wait until my education was complete and my career was established as originally planned. How would I do this? Again, with love and support, Matt and I worked out a plan.

We married in May 1987, moved in June 1987, and I began school the following fall. After 18 months of my graduate school, we decided it was time to start our family, as class work was complete and I was full-time in the laboratory working on my doctoral thesis. So, right on schedule, we became pregnant. When I told my father about my pregnancy, he again crushed me by telling me that if I had a baby, I would never finish my degrees. I vowed to myself to prove him wrong again.

A few months later, my expectant condition became obvious to the other students, faculty, and staff in my graduate department. More than one person told me that no female graduate student had ever done this before or that I was simply crazy. To me, having matured and begun to understand that life truly does happen along the way, this didn't seem so crazy. I distinctly remember sitting in a lecture with my baby kicking me in the ribs, listening to a well-respected female full professor talk about how she had put off childbearing when she was younger and could not have children now. She told the audience that this was the biggest mistake of her life. Despite her fame and prestige in her academic field, she sincerely regretted not grabbing what life had to offer when she had the chance. I was thankful that I would not be in that situation.

Baby #1 was born in July 1989. I took her into the lab with me the first few months, carrying her in a sling. She slept in a bassinet on my desk. We could not afford childcare. When this was no longer possible, I stayed home with her during the day while Matt worked. He would come home in the evening and I would leave for the lab and work well into the night. This lasted another few months until Matt was able to moonlight on weekends to cover the cost of childcare. We made it work.

Thirteen months later, I became pregnant with baby #2. We had a window of six weeks between when I finished my PhD and an impending relocation. We decided that was the perfect time to have another baby. When I told my professor that I was expecting again, he replied, "You are a very brave woman." Hmmmm. During this pregnancy, after I had set the precedent in our department, another graduate student and a faculty member also because pregnant! It seemed other women had been waiting for someone to break the ice for women in an academic department to bear children, and they saw that it could be done.

I defended my doctoral thesis looking like an overinflated balloon and passed. One month after baby #2 was born, I received my PhD and the award for the outstanding doctoral candidate in biological sciences from the dean in a ceremony with a four-week-old on my shoulder, a 22-month-old old beside me, and a wonderful husband in the audience. I honestly cannot say of which of those I was the most proud. The graduation ceremony was a celebration of all of my life, my family, and who I am.

After graduation, we moved again, but not back to the institution where I had begun my MD/PhD program as originally planned. Matt took a faculty position elsewhere, so I applied to medical school as a transfer student and was accepted. This happened again before I finally finished. Matt and I worked together to make sure the children were well cared for when one or both of us had to be out for long hours during our medical training and practice. We had many family meals in the hospital cafeteria so we could all be together for a few minutes on days when either of us had to staff the hospital, and there were many other sacrifices as well.

Ten years elapsed from the time that I began my graduate educational plan and my two degrees were completed. But most importantly, also during those 10 years, I married my soul mate, had two beautiful children, attended four different graduate schools, relocated three times, and lived a lot of life. Because I was able to not postpone life to accord with my plan, my life goals were achieved much earlier than I thought possible. My children are raised and both away at college. I am approaching 50 years of age with all of my original goals regarding education, career, and family complete. I have the entire second half of my life ahead of me to build something entirely new and different if I so desire!

The Myth of the Timetable

"We learn to be in sync with ourselves, for ourselves, and happy with the journey we take."

by Jane Wolgemuth

At age 55, I am reinventing myself. Four months ago, monikers like banker and Rotarian would suffice. These days I am a weight-lifting, ingénue chef who sees no contradiction in self-generated high cuisine and fighting against physical bulges and mental sludges. It just becomes a glorious dance. But banker and Rotarian I am, too, with 22 and 15 years spent in customer and community service, respectively. Backing up farther, I honed most of my work ethic as a meeting planner for an international educational group in Los Angeles, long before computers, cell phones, or even fax machines! With an undergraduate degree from über-liberal UC Santa Cruz and a graduate degree from ultratraditional University of Sussex, England, I settled into what women did in the '70s—found interesting, if not lucrative, work until marriage and motherhood took hold. Except in my case, motherhood instincts eluded me, and I didn't marry until I was 48. Seven years into my happy marriage, I am discovering a whole world of the unexpected and goofy talents I am now cultivating, and getting younger every day.

If you grew up as I did, in a conventional educational structure of K through12, followed by some combination of work and more schooling, then you dutifully followed the timetable set by the board of education, your parents, and society in general. No wonder that when we were set free from that institutional clock, we inadvertently created our own internal timetable—an age by which we should be married and have children; have found our lifelong partner and adopted; and bought a house/leased a condo/built a geodome in the mountains, and all usually by the age of 27.

Why 27?

I am not making this up. Nor am I talking about the biological tick-tock here, and you know it. Twenty-seven is a turning-point age through which we either make it to the other side unscathed or suffer the curse of the self-imposed timetable: we rush into life experiences because, after all, all our friends are getting married/having their first child/ publishing their first book *and if I don't join this crowd, and soon, I will never have what I want. Not ever. The train will leave the station without me on it. Everyone knows there's only one train and I cannot miss it.*

When I was 27, I saw myself being left behind in the singlehood meadow of spinsterhood; childless, loveless. All around me were new mothers, bridal showers I hosted, and those god-awful bridesmaid dresses hung in a never-visited part of my closet, and questions at family gatherings about my future (read "making grandparents out of Mom and Dad"). The cycle of life was spiraling out of control, so I found a guy to marry. So what if he was a liar, disrespectful to all, and not warm and fuzzy with my friends. I held on (more like gripped tightly, like a little kid holding a kitten by the throat) to the belief that any guy was better than no guy, that married was better than single, that my own timetable was about to out me as a failure if I didn't act fast. Not act smartly, or act reasonably, or act for the long haul, or act for anything but reaching age 28 with something!

You can see this.

But then...slowly...it occurred to me that settling for something became settling for anything. Anything soon became nothing. I woke up to the fact that I would be headed for misery and probable divorce and then misery again if I followed this colossally stupid chain of events. I wondered where I had managed to be duped by the timetable theory. Guys don't struggle with this nonsense; they father children at 81, what's the rush? It is a part of human nature, I imagine, that has us want to be in sync with our friends—up until this point, we have been in sync, starting our periods, surviving middle school, dating, and starting first jobs—and now we have to measure the worth of the who we are, and just as importantly, *when* we are. We learn to be in sync with ourselves, for ourselves, and happy with the journey we take.

Needless to say, I broke up gleefully with said guy and timetable simultaneously, and never looked back. I married for true love at age 48.

Spinning Plates

"That crisis had to happen to open me up. Without the crisis, without that plate shattering beyond all hope, I would have stayed stuck who and where I was."

by Shelly Valdez

Shelly Valdez is co-founder of M Plus Solutions Consulting, specializing in leadership and program development and evaluation. She has developed and grown programs with the United States Marine Corps, the United States Navy, the Salk Institute, and several education and corporate organizations. Under her birth name (Marks) as well as her married name, Shelly has authored and co-authored several stories, chapters, articles, and books. She can be reached at smvaldez@ cox.net.

I grew up watching *The Ed Sullivan Show*. For those not old enough to remember, it was a variety show that featured a different set of guests every week: musicians (from The Beatles and The Jackson Five to opera singers and violinists), ventriloquists, puppets, comedians, and novelty acts. Sort of like *America's Got Talent* but with professional performers and no judges. Or like *David Letterman* but with no couch.

There were several performers who were on the show repeatedly over the years. One was a man whose act involved plates. It doesn't sound exciting, but it was filled with a certain drama. He balanced a series of plates, each spinning atop its own vertical wooden stick. He ran from one place to another to keep them from falling, running back and forth along that line of wooden sticks to re-spin the wobbly ones, all to the accompaniment of fast-paced music. Always that same frenetic tune, always rushing from one end of the stick line to the other, trying, usually successfully, to keep the plates from crashing to the floor. It sounds like a silly act, but it was mesmerizing. I grew up watching those plates and that man frantically trying to keep them from shattering. In the end, he'd take them all down one at a time, stack them up neatly, and bow to great applause. I so identified with that act, it became the metaphor for my life. I referred to it often.

Fast-forward many, many years. I am not on TV and my "plates" are not china but jobs, tasks, and people. But the metaphor held. For decades, I identified with that man and felt so deeply that if I could only keep all those plates up in the air spinning, in the end, I too would be able to bow to great applause. I was keeping up a frantic musical life pace, trying to balance a whole series of plates: marriage, family, friends, career, finances, health, making this person happy, taking care of that person.

"How do you do it all?" people would ask me admiringly as I took on more and more. I am the past president, secretary, treasurer, historian, you name it of every organization I ever joined (and there were plenty), and have been known to work three jobs and two volunteer positions at once while going to school and trying to raise a family. And it was always that admiring question, that bowing to the applause of others, that kept it going.

But there eventually came a price, as I drove myself (and others) crazy. There is, as always with crazy behavior, payback. Health, peace of mind, relationships—all those plates began wobbling, and some went crashing to the floor. Still, it's hard to give up the metaphor of one's life even in the midst of watching the pieces fall around you. How do you change the metaphor so you can change the behavior? I remember sobbing to my friend Jordan one day about being like the man on *Ed Sullivan* spinning plates. Bless his heart, Jordan said, "But Shelly, he didn't have a choice and he didn't have help. You do." Simple sentences. Obvious message. But it struck me like a bolt of lightning, and thankfully the metaphor began to crumble as I learned to reframe it into a healthier one for my life and me. Here is what I now think of those spinning plates, and here is what I wish I had thought of and realized and lived a long time ago:

That man on *The Ed Sullivan Show* spun those plates for a living. I do not have to spin plates to live and it is no way to be *alive*. Taken on a small scale, it's called multitasking. We do it all the time. Driving while talking on the phone (hands free of course). Exercising while watching TV. Making dinner while monitoring homework while answering the door while feeding the baby. And all the tasks get done, BUT there are more accidents while people are on the phone (even hands free), and research is now showing that exercise is not as effective if done in front of the TV, and if I am talking to someone next to me and cutting carrots at the same time, the person I am talking to gets less of me (and I get less of the conversation) and I am likely to get cut, figuratively and literally.

Taken a step bigger, when my mind is balancing all kinds of plates at once, not one of those tasks gets my full attention, and which one does not deserve it? When working all those jobs and volunteer positions and trying to do and have it all, who or what should I sacrifice when it comes to *quality time*? My children? My husband? My health? Ironically, those looking from the outside thought I had it all. Those stroking my ego with their "How do you do it all" comments didn't see all the wobbly plates or my exhaustion. They just saw numbers and the "act."

So guess what—I learned that I could put down some plates. I learned I had choices about which ones to put down and I learned that when I did put down some plates, not only did the world not stop but also the people I cared about were happy that I had. They had my full attention when they had it and I got to have pieces of myself back, and that made me more able to *be there* when I was with them, and you can see how it goes. I do miss some (not all) of the plates I put down. But I realized they are merely placed off the sticks, not shattered, so if time and energy and desire all get to the right place, I can take them up again. In the meantime, although I miss them, I must admit to a measure of relief.

Jordan's words about help also rang true. I hadn't wanted to appear less than capable, less than independent, less than "strong," so I tried to handle all those plates myself. Such a waste, and so ironic because trying to do it all didn't make me strong, it sapped my strength. And I was depriving others of the right to do for themselves and of the gift of the feeling that comes from doing for others that I was hogging for myself.

But here's the hardest thing I had to change as I began to unravel the metaphor: It is okay for some of the plates to break! I had thought my job as wife, mother, employee, friend, you name it, was to keep everything under control to avert disaster. But as counterintuitive as it feels, sometimes crises have to happen. In fact, sometimes it is more disastrous to stop what I think is a crisis than to let it occur. Sometimes the crisis is what is necessary to move forward. In my previous marriage, for instance, I tried to avert the crisis of divorce. When my husband said he wanted to leave, I tried harder to keep the marriage together. But the disastrous end of that marriage led to amazing blessings. I went back to school and got my doctorate to better support myself and found a terrific job. I got a black belt in karate to better protect myself and found a physical strength I didn't know I had. I allowed myself to learn to like who I was alone and as a single person and then when I wasn't looking for it, found the incredible, wonderful man to whom I am now married. That crisis had to happen to open me up. Without the crisis, without that plate shattering beyond all hope, I would have stayed stuck who and where I was— running myself ragged spinning plates I no longer cared about and losing who I was in the frantic music that was then my life.

Oh, sometimes I forget and pick up too many plates, but a few months ago I accidentally broke a beautiful hand-painted Talavera plate from my collection (another irony that I would choose plates to collect, however beautiful they might be…). I had originally intended to glue it back together, but it has sat on my kitchen windowsill for months in its broken condition. I now think I will keep it in its present shape as a reminder.

Living Real Life in Ordinary Time

"Every time I left the house, it reminded me that right now was the time to be living life to the fullest, that I didn't need to be waiting for my real life to begin—the time was now!"

by Dayanne Izminan

Dayanne Izmirian, PhD, has worked as an administrator and teacher in higher education for 15 years, in both New York and California. She lives in Southern California with her family, including two young sons. She also serves on the board of directors for a local community center and enjoys cooking, reading, and crafts in her spare time.

When I was entering my mid-20s, I was living in a large apartment by myself and had the start of a great career, as I was beginning the third year of my first professional job in higher education. When I reflect back on that time, I was fairly happy, yet not truly contented. I was in a constant state of planning the future and wondering what was next. I was essentially waiting for my "real life" to begin, rather than realizing that my real life was happening now, at this very moment. Real life was unfolding on a daily basis, and through my constant anticipation of the future,

I was missing out on the wonderful everyday moments and experiences and failing to fully invest in my present situation and personal development.

Let me give you some examples of how I was waiting for my "real life" to begin. I furnished my apartment like a glorified dorm room and didn't take the time to truly make it into a home for myself. I didn't value my own space enough to make sure it was a comfortable, livable place in which I would want to spend significant amounts of time. I thought I needed to hold off on purchasing nicer items for my home until I had a bridal shower, or could afford to buy a home. I wasn't job searching aggressively, as it might mean making a move to another part of the country, and there was no way I could even fathom doing that by myself!

One day during that time (about 15 years ago now), my sister shared an article with me that changed my outlook and made a profound impact on how I began to cultivate my daily life. I cannot remember the name of the article or even the magazine in which she found it, but I will always retain the essence of its content. The author discussed how young women tend to delay their real life, waiting for weddings, children, finding a life partner, or using any other excuse they may have, rather than taking the time and energy to invest in their current situation and make the most of the present moment. I identified a great deal with what the author was saying and realized that I was in an almost constant waiting mode.

After reading the article, I was inspired to place a sign right on the inside of my front door that said "Real Life" in big, bold letters. Every time I left the house, it reminded me that right now was the time to be living life to the fullest, that I didn't need to be waiting for my real life to begin—the time was now! I started balancing my present-moment desires with future planning, rather than always looking toward the future. Soon after placing this sign on my door, I took advantage of opportunities to make my house a home and began to travel a little on my own. I had always enjoyed domestic arts such as crafts and cooking, and began to invest in some classes, some nicer-quality home items, and all those things that made my living space more comfortable and gave me hobbies that were satisfying. As I fostered a better home environment, I became more comfortable and grounded and didn't always need to be looking for something or someone else. And as an additional benefit, through my interests, I met more people and made some great friends and mentors in the process.

The "Real Life" sign on my door reminded me to keep managing that delicate balancing act of being in the present while also planning for the future in productive ways. A very practical example of this, in economic terms, is that I started putting as much away toward retirement as I could as soon as I landed my first benefits-based position. I got used to having only a certain amount of income to spend on a daily basis, and didn't even miss the money that was making its way into my long-term savings. My retirement funds were growing, and I continued to live within my means.

Within two years, the concept of living real life took on a new nuance for me, as the smaller investments I had been making in myself led to greater confidence in my abilities, and I was inspired to take bigger risks. I had always wanted to live in California, even though I had been living in upstate New York my entire life and was surrounded by my family and longtime friends. I decided that I could give California living a try, even though it would mean moving all by myself to a new city, where I knew no one. I applied for a job in San Diego, and after interviewing on-site, fell in love with the city and really admired the potential colleagues who interviewed me. Still, I prayed I would not get a job offer, as I knew I would be compelled to accept it and was overwhelmed by what this would mean for me, personally and professionally. I was offered the job, did make the cross-country move, and have been in San Diego ever since. The whole process was overwhelming and daunting, but I balanced this with careful preparation and planning and was able to make the transition as smooth as possible.

I no longer have that sign on my front door, because the idea of real life has truly taken hold in my present situation of balancing a full-time career with a full-time family. Real life has morphed into a concept of living that I now think of as making the most of Ordinary Time. This concept emerges from my personal religious upbringing, and has proven to be a very important analogy for my very busy, very full life. Basically, Ordinary Time encompasses that part of the church's year that does not fall within the special celebratory seasons of Advent, Christmas, Lent, or Easter. Since Ordinary Time runs either 33 or 34 weeks, depending on the year, it encompasses the majority of time as measured by the 52-week calendar year. In the church, Ordinary Time does not need to be ordinary—quite the opposite is true. Ordinary Time celebrates the mystery of our faith in all its aspects. Many smaller and still important liturgical celebrations fall during Ordinary Time (www. churchyear.net/ordinary.html).

There can be monotony to daily life and everyday tasks, especially when we are rushed while trying to get everything done and fitting it all in. Often, routines can be comforting, but they can also be a bit boring and unsatisfying, especially if you are not intentional about being present and making purposeful use of your time. Not every day can or needs to be a holiday, but every day can be special. It's easy to celebrate and make time for festivities during a holiday season, and so the trick is to build that same sense of fun and wonder into every minute that you can. The everyday rituals I attempt to use at home are simple ones—sitting down together for a meal, reading a favorite book to our children, and watching the sunset.

The concept of Ordinary Time is holistic in nature and encourages me to nurture all aspects of living—spiritual, emotional, and physical. Making the most of every moment does not have to be exhausting or daunting—quite the opposite. For me, it means that I choose what's important and try to keep it simple. For example, I love gardening and all that it entails. Watching something grow and transform can fill me with a great sense of wonderment and peace. It is also great fun to do with our young sons. However, having a garden is a lot of work, so to keep it simple, I use small container gardens that need a lot less work and no weeding. This fits our current lifestyle better and is not too cumbersome. Also, we love to cook in our house, and there are lots of ways to make simple and satisfying meals. If a recipe has too many steps or seems too complicated, then I simply don't make it! A final example is that it is very difficult for me to work out every day, so I try to walk our dog for 15 to 20 minutes each morning. If I can do more, that's great, but when tasks are too complicated or cumbersome, they can lose a lot of their joy and become a burden.

Living in Ordinary Time and making the most of everyday living requires a heightened sense of humor and playfulness. Although it is difficult, it is important to not take life too seriously and try to find humor and optimism when and where you can. The best way I have found to do this is to find great mentors and friends, in whose company I can be relaxed and enjoy the passing of time. Ideally, these same friends are also the ones who hold me accountable when my stress gets too high, or I am not behaving in ways that are life-giving to those around me. And of course, in real life there are some seriously tough times, and these same friends and family are the ones who support me and hold my hand during those moments of great sadness and pain. Finding a strong sense of community and companionship has been a very important way for me to create meaning and normalize the experiences and feelings of every day. As I discuss and process ideas and aggravations with others, I gain great insight into how to do things differently, or even how I may be causing my own problems!

Even though we are very busy, I try very hard to be present in every moment and for those closest to me on a daily basis—not an easy task and something I will never perfect, but well worth the effort. Repeatedly thinking to myself "Ordinary Time" and using this as a daily mantra helps keep me focused and centered, making me a better person overall. I look for opportunities to nurture my sense of purpose and spirit so I can find my own inner strength and be of service to others, assisting those around me in their own journeys as well.

Redemption

"Hands up! This fight is mine, right! I had no doubt; no ghost! He's gone, the ghost is gone! Pure joy, absolute pure joy."
by Lisa Macon

A proud mother and wife, Lisa is currently holding a position as a probation officer.

Sometimes you just have to go out and take it. For every time you second-guessed yourself. For every time others labeled you, thought they knew you, judged you, made assumptions about you and diminished you. For every heartache, loss, plan unfinished, decision you regretted, silent tear, or lonely day. When you wake up and realize that all your life everything has been "almost right." When you wish you'd had just one last day with your father, any day. Not even a graduation day, Father's Day, or wedding day, just any plain ol' day, as long as he was there. When you realize that having a career does not make you full and that finding a husband is not the finish line. The time has come to go out and paint a picture of you, painted from the inside of a conditioned body, mind, and heart. It is time to wash away the ghosts of the past and that voice inside your head. That voice that tells you, "I'm not ready," "Am I sure that's right?," "Will he like me if I say that?" The ghosts that have been haunting you since you were a little girl, a teenager, a college student, a young woman, and the woman you are today. When do they stop? Do they stop when I'm middle-aged woman? Do they stop when I'm an old woman? *No!* They stop when I wash them away.

The ghosts who whisper to me that my hair needs to be silkier, my eyelashes longer, and my hips slimmer. The ghosts who speak to me about self-doubt; who seem to always want to have a conference after a long day at work. The ghosts who scream at me that I'm not where I should be in my 30s. Those ghosts are gregarious... time to wash them away.

Jab, jab, jab, cross, hook...breath...weave...hook, hook, uppercut...wash, wash, wash...scrub, scrub. Boxing washes away the ghosts. Boxing clears the mind and revives the soul. There is vulnerability in boxing that is not found anywhere else. You are vulnerable to yourself, your trainer, your partner, your opponent, and the crowd. You have to lay your heart on the line and hand it to your trainer. One day my trainer yelled, "You've got to trust me...I know fight!" My response to that was "I don't trust men!" Here I was, sweating it out with this man every day. He showed up after a day at Sea World for his son's birthday, on his wedding anniversary, when he had a hard day at work, and I had the nerve to tell him that I "didn't trust men." After we had a snicker about my comment, it was back to training. With extra rounds of course, most likely a result of the men-and-trust comment. But did I trust myself? At that point I still didn't know. Boxing parallels life; you fight how you live.

Your trainers and training partners have to be trusted. You trust them with your time, your body, and your health. Nothing can break a friendship that's bonded by blood, bruises, and breaks...literally. I used to envy men's bonding abilities. I thought it was not fair that when girlfriends bond, they go for a coffee or a drink and basically talk about who has it worse. Guys got to do the cool stuff...football, baseball, mud runs...they built friendships that were tried and true. How tried is a female friendship that is rooted on misery loving company? Try a female friendship developed through punches,drills, water bottle sharing, yelling, and pain. That's a tried-and-true friendship, unbreakable. Family.

When people find out I box, I learn more about them than they think they've just learned about me. Most people say something like "You don't look like a boxer," or "Aren't you scared of getting hurt?" Or my personal favorite, "You mean you really box?" This question is of course accompanied with the person throwing a small flurry of poorly thrown punches in the air. I used to get offended, then I thought it was funny, and now I just realize that really it's not about me, it's about the person asking the question. He's expressing more about himself than he is about women, or me in general. That's okay; I'll prove him wrong when I fight.

Fight night is here. I prefer to think of it as my prom night, since I didn't go to my prom. The night you look so forward to, the night where plans and dreams come to fruition. I can feel my satin shorts brushing against my legs. The colors of the American flag, my heart racing, the audience screaming. Where's my robe? I need my hood; I'm still vulnerable. Okay, robe on, hood up... breathe. Why am I doing this? The ghost is back. *Jab, Jab, cross, cross, hook.* My team surrounding me, reminding me to go out and take it; don't let someone else rob you of anything that you worked for. Don't let my work with my team be in vain. Go prove to everyone watching that they don't know me. Their assumptions are wrong; my past is just that, my past. I hear the first few notes of my entry song, the smoke starts to rise in the air around me, the lights flash. My hands, each an extra 14 ounces heavier, on my trainer's shoulders are about to go to work. He's in front of me, facing the crowd ahead of me, protecting his fighter, taking care of his fighter, framing his fighter. My team behind me has my back. I'm introduced, the crowd cheers, my heart is beating fast; *breathe, breathe...jab, jab, jab.* Eyes focused, hood up, walking through the crowd, still vulnerable. Extra vulnerable...supersized vulnerable!

The three stairs to the ring are like the stairway to heaven...or hell? Climbing through the ropes, I feel the padded canvas under my feet. I take one lap around the ring, slowing down just in time to stare at my opponent in her corner. She wants none of this...right? Ghosts. Back to my trainer. Robe off. Mouthpiece in. Last-minute instructions; keep that jab going, right hands, bang to the body, lift her up. My trainer steps out...vulnerable. He's gone, like the ghosts. I'm alone in here, with a girl who wants to rip my head off, and how many thousand people screaming and watching? The bell rings.

Jab, jab, jab, right. Keep punching. The punches land. She lands a right hand. That's it? I can take that! I can take that! *Jab, jab, right, left uppercut. Combos.* Keep pushing, keep pressing. She's backing off. Go out and take it, take her heart. She gets a standing eight-count…look toward my corner. Okay, my trainer, thank God! I see him: *jab, jab, jab, right, hook, uppercut.* Okay, go do it. I can do it. I do it. I trust him! I trust me. Bell rings, round one over. The crowd is screaming; I'm in the corner. Water and instructions, and breathe.

Round two. *Jab, jab, jab,* it all works off the jab. My opponent tries to come out hard. I can take it. I tasted it and I got this. Push through it. Keep the combos coming. Her trainer is yelling to her, "She's tired!" No I'm not! He does not know me; he does not know what I've done to get here. How dare he scream to her that I'm tired! Extra combos coming for her. Bell rings, round two over. The crowd is screaming; I'm in the corner. Water and instructions, and breathe. Oh, and he wants more from me. He's yelling— great, more yelling.

Round three. She's running. *Dig deep. Push the fight, push, push, push. Body, body, body, head, head. Mix it up, combos.* I hear my trainer. Thirty seconds left, *go, go, go, go take it!* Pounding on the mat, 10 seconds left. Leave it all out here, every bit of doubt, loss, and fear. Bell rings. Round over.

Hands up! This fight is mine, right! I had no doubt; no ghost! He's gone, the ghost is gone! Pure joy, absolute pure joy. No weight on my shoulders, no worry, no twisting thoughts. Just me, sweaty and out of breath, and my trainer. Cutting the wraps off my hands, telling me it was my fight. Oh and the crowd; *the crowd!* Finally, something is just right! And I worked for it. No luck, no chance, no roll of the dice. And now for the decision… "Fighting out of the blue corner…!" My hand is raised and I jump around. I trust me.

There are very few things in life that give back what you put into them. I can put 100 percent into my work, but I'm not going to get it back. I can put my heart into my family, but unfortunately I'm not going to get it all back. Whatever you put into boxing, you will get back. If you put in the work, honest, hard, and tough, you will get it back. Morning runs, grueling afternoon workouts, and tons of punches are part of the equation. But there was more. I realized I had to focus and just "do me." After I quit trying to be like other fighters, I found myself. I used to watch other fighters and try and emulate them, to try and be like them. I finally realized that I couldn't be like them. Like my trainer said, "God sprinkled special powder on you; you're 75 percent puncher and 25 percent boxer." Really? The way I am is okay? We can work with this? I know that my job was to "do me," work hard, and to listen. His job was to water my strengths so they would grow; not to change them into something that could never be.

I love boxing. I now know why. It's my equation for life. Boxing has helped me find me, trust me, believe in me. Today the ghosts are gone. Tomorrow they may try and come back but I have boxing, my ghost buster! Silence in my head happens, finally!

If I live life the way I box, I'll live full. *Jab, jab, jab.* I have to jab, just stick it out there, hard and fast, measure it out. It all works off the jab. The jab sets up everything, the right hand, left hook, and uppercut. Without the jab, they don't work. No matter what happens you have to keep going, just like the jab. Then you can throw the power shots. Jab to make it to the big events. The moments you hope for and dream of. The power punches. The sunny days off, a good sermon at church, summer rain, the smell of the ocean, puppy breath, weddings, babies, a new house. Those are the power punches, the "good stuff." But without the jab, or the inner fire and hope to just keep it going, the power punches never happen. Without belief in me, the sunny days or power punches aren't as powerful. I've learned that although those punches may not always land, at least you are throwing them and if you stay committed, eventually they will land.

We've all heard the saying "roll with the punches." I say, "Keep throwin' that jab!" I don't want to live to roll through someone else's punches. I want to throw my own. Throw those jabs to set up the moments. The moments we treasure may be sneaky and we may never see them coming, but they sure are powerful. Sometimes you have to just go out and take it, and wash away those ghosts, champ.

You Should Have Listened to Your Mother

"You've heard it before and it bears repeating: if it's meant to be now, it will be meant to be next year. Slow down."

By Stephanie Peck Hall

Stephanie Peck Hall is a married mother of two from Laguna Hills, California. She is co-author of the book, The Psychic Next Door, and works full time as the Vice President of Marketing for Los Angeles-based CompuLaw LLC. Her most important job, however, is as a caretaker for her son, Ethan, 6, and her daughter, Sarah Elaine, 3. She can be reached at stpeck@cox.net.

I'm sorry, but someone had to say it out loud. You should have listened to your mother.

I had a great mom. She was the most dedicated, selfless mother that ever walked the earth. This woman would eagerly listen to my phone chatter, oftentimes through my entire drive home from work (and I live in Southern California). She would take my calls at all hours and welcome my visits whenever I came through her door. She would escort me to the mall, or even the grocery store and the dreaded doctor's appointment, whenever, always with a listening ear. During our conversations, mom would delicately offer her support and then gently offer her advice. She never pushed me to make any decisions or to choose her point of view (except politically, she was a tried and true Democrat). Sometimes, I took her advice. Most of the time, I did not.

Now, my mom wasn't exactly the most typical mother. She was a redheaded, fiery Italian woman, and quite beautiful too. She never had much trouble attracting men, even into her late sixties! And even more intriguing, she was a psychic. No, not the kind you pay $5 for at the fair. My mom took private clients in her home office and did not advertise her services. Referrals came strictly by word of mouth, and she charged a pretty penny to offer spiritual advice.

My mom, Elaine S. Peck (yes, her real initials were ESP), had quite a delivery for her information. She was a Jersey City, New Jersey native, cussed like a sailor and sure wasn't afraid to tell you what was on her mind. She was a colorful character, and often very funny. Many, many times, I'd watch from the distance as my mom captivated an entire room with her entertaining banter. She was so much fun!

Even still, as the daughter of a psychic that was filled with valuable insight, I didn't always take her advice. I suppose it's normal, even healthy, to want to go your own way. Besides, intimate relationships are so very personal that we often tell ourselves that no one can truly understand our unique situation. And although some moms are caring and concerned (mine was, though I realize some are not), we tend to believe that we know what's best for ourselves. We gather all of the advice (or the insults), and then we make our own decision. Thanks for the talk. Thanks for the strength. Now, "I" know what to do.

What's wrong with us? Mom's have some really great information to share! Looking back on my life, I now wish I had listened to my mom more often. Like most girls, my mom had her own favorite set of "momisms" to offer me. You know, the phrases and clichés passed down from a mother to her unappreciative children. Some of them are funny. Some of them are poignant. Some of them are impossible to understand (but that's a whole 'nother Oprah). And, unfortunately, like it did for me, it often takes becoming a mom ourselves before we finally realize the wisdom of our own mother's advice.

Now a married woman with two young children, I myself can look back (and kick myself) for missing the gems of wisdom my mom offered to me in my youth. "Youth is wasted on the young," she used to tell me. Well, it doesn't have to be.

<u>Know Him for One Year</u>

"What's the rush?" she used to ask (followed by a "G.D." or some other foul expletive). Why do so many women label the new guy as "it" and rush to make permanent plans? Is it that they are afraid that their partner may discover them to be someone they're not? That they believe if they move in together or marry him now, it will solidify the relationship? Or, is it because they believe the permanence proves that their partner's level of commitment is real?

Whether the answer is yes or no, all of these insecurities make not a reason to trust that the relationship is commitment-worthy. Like mom would say, people DO change over the course of the year, that's why you should heed this advice. The way folks interact with their families during the holidays is much different than the way that this special someone interacts alone with you during private time at the pool in the summer months. During a twelve month period, you may overcome a hardship together, witness a miracle, whether a tragedy – who knows. Whatever happens, you learn more about the person you're with and discover if, indeed, this relationship can handle the natural ups and downs of life! You've heard it before and it bears repeating: if it's meant to be now, it will be meant to be next year. Slow down.

He's Italian Catholic! He Will Never Leave His Wife!

You know who you are. You're the smart, practical, level-headed woman that has convinced herself that his relationship with that other woman is due to circumstances beyond his control. You've told yourself that it's only a matter of time before he lets go of that wife, ex-wife, ex-girlfriend, friend, whatever—and puts all of his focus on you. There's always a good reason there to explain why he spends so much of his time and energy on this woman, and you swallow it because the alone time you two have proves that he cares about you the most.

"Wake up!" Elaine would offer you no mercy. If you're not number one today, you will not be number one tomorrow. Good men with good love to share don't pass it around like a football. You want a man, no, you deserve a man that loves only you! If he can't make a clean break with the "other" person, there's something wrong with him. Be strong and move on.

Look to His Mother

(It might come out "mutha") My mom used to say, "look at how he treats his mother. The way he treats her is the way he will ultimately treat you." For some gals, this is good news. A lot of men are wonderful to their moms. They buy flowers on Mother's Day and call mom whenever they have important news to share. If mom needs help or support, they are there to offer it both physically and emotionally. When mom needs a shoulder, he has two. Now, I'm not talking about a fanatical momma's boy (see section above), I'm talking about a good, decent, caring son. This is the guy you want.

However, if you're in a relationship with the guy that forgets his mother, or, worse still, lies to his mother … run, don't walk. What does it say about the deeper familial bond this man's life has been built on if he doesn't care about his own mom. Yes, of course, some moms frankly deserve to be avoided, but that's pretty rare. As far as mom's go, you get what you get, and you're generally a happier, more stable person if your mother/son (or, mother/daughter) relationship is intact. Watch your guy's behavior and attitude towards his mom. Listen to the way he talks about her. Observe the interaction. Then, make the right decision for yourself.

Marry a Friend, Not a Lover

Think for a moment about the couples that have survived thirty-plus years of marriage. Rarely do you find a relationship like that of my Aunt Virgie and my Uncle Sam—the happily ever after we all wish for. They were married for over sixty years and never spoke an ugly word to each other. She called him her "dude," and her "man." He looked at her, even in old age, as if she were an angel handed down from God.

Unfortunately, most couples have to work a little harder than Aunt Virgie and Uncle Sam and suffer some pretty dramatic ups and downs in their lives, especially if they share children. Once you get married, you don't stop growing up (well, most of us don't). You continue to share new experiences that enrich your lives, and these experiences change you.

Mom would remind me, with lovers that "complete you," you're counting on them, well, to be there for you. Sometimes, folks forget that the relationship you have really isn't "together as one," it is a relationship made up of two different people that continually choose to tread through life together. If this relationship is based on love and passion only, the fuel that flames the fire could die out. Then, what are you left with?

If, however, you marry a friend, you have the possibility to really, truly be happy. Friends are kind to each other. They support each other in their own, individual dreams. They know how to listen and they know how to share. They know how to give and not just to need. Friends laugh, and friends fight. Friends agree, and friends disagree. But, the strength of the relationship is the joy that comes from the bond that is created over the course of time. An enduring relationship grows out of true friendship, not passion. Do not mistake the fervor that attracts you to a person in the first place as the foundation for a lasting marriage.

<u>Feed the Man First</u>

At my niece's wedding shower, we played a little game. All the ladies stood together in a circle, holding a candle. As their candle was lighted, each woman offered some advice to the bride-to-be. When the flame came towards my mom, we were all anxious to hear what she would say. Her words? "Feed the man first."

Yes, she got a good laugh out of that, but I have been surprised at how often women quote her statement still today. It's not just about filling his empty belly up with food, it's so much more. It's about satisfying his simple needs first. It's about giving of yourself before taking. It's about letting go of the fight to be right, to be first, to be independent. It's okay sometimes not to be the strong woman in charge, and just to be his girl. Sometimes, we modern woman get in our own way. We don't want to take his name. We want our own careers and our own night's out. Okay, but make sure you soften yourself too, and give yourself up to the relationship. You might be surprised at how happy it makes you too.

<u>If You're Walking Down the Aisle and You Change Your Mind, It Will be Okay with Me</u>

To me, this was the sweetest, most loving advice my mom could ever offer to me. She wasn't trying to tell me that she didn't support my marriage, she was just trying to tell me that she loved me, unconditionally. That she was there for me, no matter what. And, I tell you now, there is nothing like the love and the support of your mom when the time comes for you to commit yourself to love.

I lost my mom in 2004. Well, we all lost my mom.

Although my sisters do their best to provide me with their own morsels of mind, I still hear my mom's words often.

Yes. She loved you first, as they say. She knows best. So, listen well. Someday, if you're lucky, you will have the blessed opportunity to pay it forward.

I Choose to Thrive

"All the while I kept telling myself: I am bigger than this moment."

by Minoshia Gail Humphrey

Since 1985, Minoshia Gail Humphrey has worked on a subtle energy level guiding people toward reconnecting any global and local disconnects. Minoshia resides in the Laguna Beach, California area and will move to be around any and all grandchildren. She can be contacted; minoshia11@aol.com; www.instantmindshift.com; www.blogtalkradio.com//minoshiahumphrey.

I will be 55 years old on August 1, 2009. I am a female born in Kinston, North Carolina, who originally lived over a little downtown shoe shop. Our front window view was of train tracks where tobacco was shipped daily, and our back view overlooked a steepled church. I played on a corrugated steel roof in the heat, humidity, and freezing cold. My real father was born in 1899 and married my real mother when she was 43 and he was 67. I was placed with my step sister and her husband and adopted in Fort Wayne, Indiana, at the age of three and a half. The reason I was placed outside of my home has yet to be truly explained, and most of my relatives are dead now or never spoke the truth when asked. My stepsister—same mom, different dad—had been charged with deserting her own son and never found him, although she searched and searched. How she was allowed to adopt anyone was and is beyond me. My greatest lessons in kindness were learned from Buddy Lee Clifton, deceased, and my greatest lesson in compassion was taught by Clara Leigh Clifton, who died in 2009.

I choose to inspire people with a belief system called Taking Creative Action Gives You Traction Today. Here's why: I was left on a doorstep at the age of three and a half. I was given money so I would stop crying, as my mother drove away in a cab and left me with strangers in a *very* unfamiliar place. Left to adjust and survive on my own with no other resources than a three-year-old has. It wasn't that it was done—it was how it was done. I cannot remember meeting either of these people except for once, when the adoptive woman and my real dad argued in our house. Soon she was the new mom that I never warmed to. The new people tried their best on military pay to provide for and raise me in a house with a pond in the backyard in Indiana. If I had ever been given a choice, would I be better adjusted today? I will never know. I do know that I know the dark side of adoption. My face was beaten black and blue, and the lie at school was that I fell. It did not stop there, and the abuse only ended the day I walked out.

Buddy never left me alone with Clara again without checking in frequently. The forms of abuse were numerous and painful, both mentally and emotionally. I was supposedly chosen for adoption, so I was special, but I never felt that way. I have chosen to have a wonderful adulthood because there was nothing I could do about my childhood.

When I turned 18, I left my home with my best friend's help at 6:30 in the morning. I looked forward to the wonderfulness that I could create in my future. I began discovering my likes, dislikes, opinions, and preferences and took action in all aspects of my life. I cannot say the journey has been all straight and narrow, but the adventures were relished and archived to play in my memory. I began traveling, exploring other cultures, faiths, and interests. I inherited some money at the age of 19, got a brand-new car, and left Barstow, California, the town where I was brought up. I enrolled at Sacramento State University in 1976, where I majored in Journalism, with a minor in Business Administration and a concentration in Human Resources, and graduated in 1979. I went to school on Social Security and VA benefits because by now my adopted dad had passed away. Later, I also took 30 units in child development. I realized along the way that I had emotional problems that interfered with my ability to focus, and I took action to address and clear any and all issues that blocked my progress. All the while I kept telling myself: I am bigger than this moment.

I have been in pursuit of happiness since 1985. I discovered how to use the gift I was given. I work on a subtle energy level, helping people reconnect any disconnects in their lives. It has been both a blessing and a curse—a blessing because it has helped a lot of people; a curse because I did not at first quite know how to monetize this ability or turn it into a viable business. As the clearing of my own emotional issues increased, the power of the gift got stronger.

I have now found my niche. I am on radio and TV—I have my own blog talk radio show, Your Instant Mindshift + Coast to Coast Collaboration, and I love to write. Taking Creative Action Gives You Traction Today is a way of life for me. I stay focused through guided imagery and life action coaching, masterminding and checking on my feelings over and over again. I also discovered Change Your Water Change Your Life Kangen water, alkaline water that allows you to let go of the acidic waste in your body.

Finding Your Path

"Trust that you need no one other than you to give the answer. You know."

by Reina Bach

Reina Bach specializes in executive coaching, leadership and talent development, organizational change, and talent management. Reina is an adjunct faculty member with the University of Colorado Graduate School of Business, the Women's Vision Foundation, and the Western Management Development Center. She has worked with a variety of corporations, management teams, and government organizations in the United States, the UK, and Asia.

Reina earned an MA in Industrial and Organizational Psychology at the University of Colorado, a BA in Engineering with a minor in Computer Science from Lafayette College, as well as a Grande Diploma from the prestigious French Culinary Institute in New York. She is a certified leadership coach through Georgetown University and is also certified to administer a number of assessment instruments. When she's not working with organizational leaders, Reina enjoys hosting gourmet dinner parties, international leisure travel, photography, rock climbing, and golf. She can be reached at

ReinaBach.com

Answering the question "What do you wish you'd known somewhere between the ages of 20 and 35?" sounds simple, right? Not so simple. Looking back, there are *sooooo* many things I wished I'd known then. How do I narrow it down? What are those precious nuggets of wisdom that might have made life a little easier, helped me avoid (at least a few) potholes? Truth be told, there is one major nugget…

Pressure to be someone's idea of you—have you ever felt that? If so, read on. If not, you can skip this chapter. What I'm talking about is finding yourself captive in someone else's version of your life… You should be a doctor. You should get married and have kids. You should, you should, you should… Meanwhile, the essence of your true self is dying on the vine.

Back in high school, it so happened that I was good in math *and* I also loved my home economics cooking class. Do they even have home ec in high schools anymore? Johnson and Wales was calling, while the Culinary Institute of America was singing to my soul—come here, have fun, live your passion. Hmm…in the other ear was my mother saying, "Oh, but you're so good in math and science, you should be an engineer." What the heck was an en-gin-eer, and what about my culinary future? Needless to say, the decision that followed shaped the beginning of my "should" life, a façade life. I was young and easily influenced, and wanted so much to please my parents and make them proud of me. Mom wanted me to get an engineering degree, so that's what I did.

The fake life continued on through college and

afterward, when I bluffed my way as a software developer and married a fabulous guy named Kevin. The techie life was about as far away from my true self as could be. Staring at a computer screen, watching a program blow up because of a misplaced period or comma, working 22-hour days documenting the programs I'd written, in a room full of 100 programmers where all you'd hear is the clackity-clack of keyboards being tapped. Most days I wanted to stand up and scream, "Let me out!" and most nights I'd party my way through the evening with several glasses of wine to forget the day, to forget the fact that my stomachache started every Sunday night before a new workweek. I tried to numb out my life. Yet, this was the life I "should" be living. I felt so disconnected, so unsure of myself, so lost, so fragmented.

And then there was Kurt, my first husband. He was smart (Ivy League undergrad and MBA), attractive, athletic, and nice—great pedigree. We laughed a lot together—that silly kind of laughter. We had the quintessential storybook wedding—the white dress with a long, gorgeous train of handmade Italian lace, surrounded by smiling family and friends, with sunset photos by the lake, great food, and fun music. Many guests said it was the best wedding they'd ever attended. I had the wedding my mother always wanted for herself. I was the dutiful daughter.

After a year, I found myself asleep in my own life. After two more years and several therapy sessions, I woke up and walked away from the marriage. Great guy, wrong guy for me. I was in a commission-only sales job and needed cash to support myself, so I sold one of the few assets I had—my diamond wedding band and engagement ring. Moments after I sold them at a local jewelry shop, I called my mom. Her response was, "What do you mean you sold them? I wanted those rings. I would have bought them from you for myself." She immediately called the jeweler, who agreed to sell them to her at the same price they'd paid me. I was stunned.

At that point, I was completely disconnected from myself. And "finding myself" became an obsession, an addiction that lasted the next 15 years—through 30-some jobs, 20 homes, and four cross-country and one international move. Clearly, I needed help.

Starting with a more scientific approach, I took a number of "tests" designed to help me figure things out. There were (and still are) tons of assessments—some for understanding your personality type, how you work with others, what type of work environment and activities you prefer and what you're good at, and some that identify your optimal career choice. It was all so confusing—there was so much data to assimilate that I got "wrapped around the axle" mentally. OVERLOAD!

Time saver: Pull out those career tests you took in high school. They're pretty accurate!

The journey continued…birthing work with Margaret, soul retrieval with Vivian, body cleansing with Katherine, astrology charting with Carol and John, tarot cards with Elle, clairvoyant readings with Druanne, a stress workshop with Deepak Chopra, psychic readings with Maryann and Jessica, and regular visits to The Twelfth House metaphysical store, my home away from home. Sure, I'd seen psychotherapists over the years, but this was much more intriguing and engaging. Oh, almost forgot the chakra alignment, kundalini awakening, acupuncture, Chinese herbal remedies, flower therapy, meditation, body alignment energy therapy, and feng shui. Did I miss anything?

Oh yes. I also sought the wisdom and guidance of Karlton, oil tycoon by day and a crystal healer by night. Goodness, was I stunned when he could see anger in me! No, that was rage. What was I so mad about? Me—nice, sweet me—what on earth could have me so upset? But he could see my red aura floating out from my body. Yes, it was there and needed to be released. Scary! What an enlightening yet tormenting experience it was! Karlton had processed his rage years before by hacking up old furniture with a hatchet in his basement for days on end. Move over, road rage! My own solution, given that I didn't have a basement, nor old furniture, nor a hatchet, was to go into my bedroom, close the windows and doors (I didn't want the neighbors to call the police!), and beat my futon bed until I felt the red fog lift. God, that felt good—screaming, beating the bed with my Wiffle ball bat, breathing erratically, followed by moments of streaming tears. Out she came, that angry alien. Rage be gone!

Now that the rage was named and being handled, there was the whole issue of my name. Have you ever had the feeling your parents got your name wrong? How could they really know who you are? You cook in the womb for nine months and out you come, bustling out into your new playground. Ever since I was in third grade, I knew something wasn't right. I tried, I tried to be the birth name. Uh, uh. Nope. Didn't fit. So, one day in grade school (I went there for all of six months, but that's another story), I started writing *Rebekah* instead of *Rebecca*. Maybe I felt biblical inspiration being in Catholic school…or maybe I was getting glimpses into the real me. R-E-B-E-K-A-H. It felt good; I felt like I was taking back my essence and my freedom. My parents just screwed up on the name. No problem, I'll fix it. I'll take back control.

Finally, years later at the age of 31, I was sitting in a trailer meditating with friends in Boulder, Colorado. Hmmm. This name kept popping into my head—RAYNA. RAYNA. I played around with the spelling for a while. The following year, I realized that Reina didn't go with Peterson. The last name seemed rather flat. Digging deep into my synthetic roots (there was an adoption in the family tree), I settled on taking my great-great-great-grandfather's last name—Bach. Interesting to discover in third grade while doing a family-tree school project that he, the famous Johann Sebastian Bach, was in my family tree. Bringing in some of that male, get-out-there-and-do-it energy felt right. Reina Sebastian, Reina Bastien, Reina Bach. Bingo! That's me.

Two years later, I was ready to make the switch. Expecting a long, arduous process to legally change my name, I was gearing up mentally for the transformation. I remember sitting there in my car—all alone, since my closest friend was working and couldn't be there with me—crying. This was huge, changing my legal name and taking on a new identity. I was in and out of the courthouse in 20 minutes. Who knew? If more people realized how easy it was, maybe they'd change their names, too. After the legal change came all the fun with credit cards, social security, passport, et cetera. Boom, done. I went from Rebecca Anne Peterson to Reina Bach in moments. Now what? The name change was the last great stand to reclaim my real self. With the swish of a pen, I could no longer be controlled by my mother nor live the life she'd prescribed for me. So there!

The Nugget

Those 15 years were filled with lots of exploration, many glasses of wine, and way too much self-judgment. I'd go so far as to say even self-sabotage. The funny thing is that it hit me just recently that there are tons of choices out there and everyone has an opinion about what you could do with your life, what you *should* do with your life. The secret: Ask yourself what the highest expression of you is, quietly listen to what comes up—without judgment or negativity—and trust that you know who you are. Trust that you need no one other than you to give the answer. You know. Had I realized that back then, I could have saved tons of money and spared myself the self-torture and condemnation.

The true nugget of wisdom I discovered, which I finally unwrapped as I wrote these pages, is that I'd made up a story about my life—that I wasn't pursuing my passion because my mother forced me to make her choices for me and she controlled my life. I told myself that she was living her life vicariously through me and that one of her sole purposes was to run my life. In return for holding that story as the "Truth," I got to blame her and make her wrong rather than take responsibility for my own happiness. I imprisoned myself in a disempowering story that, ironically, was what held me back. That story justified the frenzied 15-year search to find my "true self," the overindulgence in red wine, the reckless and irresponsible relationship with money, and the unrest in my heart. I blamed her for my unhappiness—all of it. And that was the root of the rage uncovered in my sessions with Karlton so many years before. I kept telling myself that "things should be different, my life should be different." It was so easy to blame someone else, having started from the premise that "things should be different." The victim inside wanted to blame everyone by myself. The anguish and suffering I caused myself could have been avoided if only I'd come clean about my story. And it was only a story, my story. Not the Truth, but my truth, which I defiantly preserved just to make my mother wrong.

Now it's your turn to set yourself free. What stories are you making up about your life that keep you disempowered? Are you blaming someone else for your life not being as you want it, for your unhappiness or your discontent? If you have a story, what's the payoff to you for holding onto it? Who do you get to make wrong? Who do you get to blame? Consider that it's just your story, and a story can be rewritten.

In a conversation years later with my mother about the rings, she told me, "I didn't want your life or to control your life, and I wasn't jealous of you. I'd never had diamonds before, and I bought them because I knew I'd never afford them otherwise." I spent years being mad at her for being "controlling and envious" of my life, when in fact all she wanted was the best for me and a little bit for herself. I was so hell-bent on being right that I wasn't able to see my amazing mother.

Find your stories and let them go sooner rather than later. Forgive yourself for being human, for we are all storytellers in one way or another.

Our Inner Voice

"Communication is the way relationships begin, extend, and sustain, especially the one with one self."

By Solluna Moyoah

Solluna is a master holistic health practitioner, herbalist, minister, teacher, personal insight counselor, and Reiki master. She is specializing in the diminishing and elimination of pain: physical and mental. Her education and experiences, in the United States and abroad, focus on gaining greater knowledge of the benefits of massage while enhancing her techniques. She has a BA in Biology (University of San Diego), has medical massage and Reiki master certifications, and is a professional member of the American Massage Therapy Association and National Board for Therapeutic Massage and Bodywork and a member of Pyrysys Psychology Group. She continues to develop and refine her abilities and self. For example, she is currently conducting research about fatigue and posture. Solluna is available for workshops, seminars, and lecturing. She delights in sharing her scientific and artistic knowledge and experience, and has been providing therapeutic massage and counseling therapies for 40 year. Contact Solluna & Company Therapeutic Massage & Inspired Alchemy Spa: sollunaco@scbglobal.net.

It is an honor to be invited to participate in this exceptional project. Once asked, I considered several topics, including self-love, relationship, self-talk, trust, and acceptance. Ultimately, I came to the realization that all of these were inherent in the relationship I have with myself, which proceeds from my willingness to develop and grow. This is largely due to the most spiritual form of communications available to me, my inner voice. Communication is the way relationships begin, extend, and sustain, especially the one with one self. The ultimate relationship experience is as body, mind, soul, and spirit. When we realize the true essence of our being as an individual, it is the unity of our self.

Being born into poverty, as well as having my own poverty consciousness, I witnessed and experienced a great deal of negative energy. Even so, life brought me into the spiritual realm at an early age. I began to experience a numinous "voice" and soon came to realize it was coming from within me. Benefits from contact with my inner voice literally have become a lifesaver for me. I encountered and remember the encouragement and counsel of my elders and others from my early childhood and adulthood. Their pronouncements, and the reality of them, were akin to the following: "take heed of your first thought," "listen to your inner voice," "follow your intuition," "pay attention," "use common sense." Over time, these expressions grew into my awareness as important and impactful concepts. They guide and protect me along my life's pathways and other ways, even now. Developing the four levels of communication skills (inner voice, outer voice, listening, and boundaries) was and sometimes even now is very challenging. These skills are an evolving art- and science-requiring practice at all times.

Early on, all too often I did not listen, take heed, nor allow the voice of wisdom to speak. Too often, I did not follow my first mind. I did not trust. Over the course of my time and personal experiences, I have come to ascertain that the truth (for me) of the inner voice is all about trust in oneself, our highest purpose and attributes—named God/ Goddess and others terms considered sacred. Had I trusted even a small fraction of the occasions I was aware of my inner voice speaking to me, I truly believe I would be more successful at this period of my life. The times I was disinclined to listen were usually stressful. In that mind-set, I was doing all I could to be the one in control, instead of being in trust of my life process. Of course, those were the times I needed to be still, listen, and respond.

I question, fundamentally, what occurs—the listening or the hearing? Which one allows me the connection to myself knowing and follow-through of the inner voice guidance? The recurring adage has been to "listen to your inner voice." Whether one listens to and/or hears one's inner voice, the active ingredient is trust, which I have found results from love and acceptance; it is a process of realization happening over time and space. However, as I stepped into my self-acceptance, I realized how much more self-perspective I have to attain. My self-love came into fullness. Now, true trust is engaged in a sacred usefulness throughout the operations of my life.

My inner voice has saved me from hurt, harm, and danger, and even possibly saved my life. I was about 21 years old, on my first visit to New York, when my inner voice awakened me to divine protection. Walking alone around 2:00 a.m. on a seemingly deserted street in Harlem, Brooklyn, or Queens—I really can't recall the area—I had been abandoned by a man who didn't like the fact that I wasn't going to have sex with him. He hastily gave me some instructions about getting to the subway and disappeared. I did not have a clue as to my location when, astonishingly, I realized my inner voice was speaking, making me aware that two men were following me. The voice told me to walk tall and strong, and not run. I was protected! At the next street corner I would see why.

At that corner was a police car. I was able to stop the policemen. I told them I was lost and that I'd noticed I was being followed. It seemed the men had ducked into an alley. The policemen did not observe them; there was no proof of what I was saying. The officers informed me that all they could offer were directions to the nearest subway, several blocks away. They then drove away. Once the policemen were out of sight, my inner voice spoke, telling me to stay calm; look back; trust! As I looked back, I saw the men who'd been following me were out of the shadows and were actually running toward me. My inner voice commanded me: *Do not run! Walk strong!* This was awfully difficult. Yet, somehow, I intuited to do as guided. As I was arriving at the next corner, the same police car drove up. I was instructed to get into the car. The policemen said they'd seen my pursuers as they ran out of the shadows. Therefore, they could appropriately assist me. I was soon taken directly to my door, safe and sound. I am certain that had I done other than follow the advice and support of my inner voice, a terrible consequence would have transpired.

Most of us have or will encounter the voice of self-deprecation. This voice does not serve any positive purpose. This limiting voice is not our inner voice; at best, it is negative self-talk (another subject). In order for the pure voice of self-love, which is Spirit, to be fulfilled, a decision to become aware is imperative. We have to pause and observe our thoughts and ourselves with loving acceptance. Self-love is a sign of health and being in balance with our social surroundings and ourselves.

Lovingly giving me directions, my inner voice has stood at the entry of my awareness, leading me to choose another course of action. For instance, during a business transaction I was feeling very unsettled. I dismissed the feelings and chose to call them "excitement" about the pending business enrichment I was about to receive. I decided to misrepresent my inner voice. Consequently, I allowed a fraudulent situation to occur at a cost of $11,500. The positive side concerning this Internet fraud was character building. I also had to pay homage to the act of forgiveness to both the perpetrators and myself. This was indeed a process of character development, fine-tuning discernment, and learning to trust my inner voice.

There can be moments in time and events when it is difficult to find words to convey our experiences as our inner voice converses with us. Surely, I have experienced "heaven" opening up before my physical eyes. I was driving as this occurred. Without any forewarning, I suddenly felt completely different inside my entire body and the car's interior. I was compelled to look high toward the sky. What I saw was astonishingly beautiful and actually reflected the way I was feeling inside. I could not stop tears from flowing. I was looking at the sky's movements of colors, feeling sensations within me, and crying for about 15 minutes. I was "told" to notice the time. The next day, I was notified that my father had transitioned during the night. Later inquiring about his passage, I realized it was *exactly* the same time I was having my mystical experience. When I recall the awesomeness of the connection, it causes me tears even today. For this happening, I have an inexpressible depth of gratitude to my inner voice.

Speaking its own internal language, our inner voice is positive and speaks from love, giving us the abilities to know ourselves and transcend all obstacles, and exposing our beautiful souls. By practicing observance of our surroundings and without immediate reactions to either the ugly and/or the beautiful, we can adjust our attitudes and change our perspectives. We are given our authentic connections with our intuitions, as well as our feelings and opinions. This may assist in closing the gap of separation between us and the truth of our wholeness.

Listening and responding to my inner voice is an act of self-love. This greatly assists in avoiding, evaluating, and preventing adverse actions and emotions of being a spiritual being and having human experiences brings to my life. It aids in the non-use, misuse, and/or use of my experiences. It enables the strength and awareness to recognize the opportunities for me to create everything into blessings of goodness.

On my self-love journey, I surmised that the inner voice is a function of mind and soul. Our mind operates in our physical world for the fulfillment of our bodies and emotions. Our soul connects directly to our spiritual Source.

Self-love faith and intention of gentle praise, patience, effort, and consideration will allow us to recognize the guidance of our inner voice, directing us to all occasions for the realization of our divinity. In due course, by loving self first, being still, and honoring our inner voice, we are privileged to experience life's abundance and the joys of happiness, health, wealth, peace, and prosperity. Love is an action of directive energy, of awareness and pure aliveness.

We are all born with brilliance and the ability to conceive. In life, we tend to stop listening to our inner voice. We need to connect to our access to this extraordinary ability, to realize our holy wholeness. To tune inward to Source and hear our inner voice is the way to our harmonious, peaceful, and silent inner state. The still whisper of our self-love is a continuous state of well-being. Perhaps you have or will learn to silence everything around you. So listen and hear your inner voice. Extend your life to be for yourself and others evermore the blessings of love and light. *I love you!*

He's Not Your Best "Girlfriend"

"Invest in relationships with women whom you respect and admire."

by Beth Martinez

Beth Martinez currently lives with her family in North San Diego County. She holds a BA in Philosophy from the University of California, Irvine (1992), and an MS in Environmental Studies, with a concentration in Policy and Planning and an emphasis in Watershed Management and Conflict Resolution (2002).

Beth has been instrumentally involved in her industry for more than 12 years. She currently manages the regulatory division for an environmental consulting firm based in Orange County, California. Resolving complex multidimensional conflicts with project planning and implementation has become her area of expertise. In addition, she currently serves as a part-time faculty member at Saddleback Community College, Mission Viejo, California. She designed and instructs a class in Environmental Ethics.

I've been married nearly 10 years and have enjoyed the privilege of meeting and getting to know maybe more than my fair share of gents, so what I am about to explain comes to you with that experience. I lived my 20s as a single woman, and I really lived them. I enjoyed being single and made the very most of it. I still do my best daily to understand relationships with men, which for me now includes marriage and a young child and all that comes with it.

What I have learned, and what I really believe to be true, is that relationships are hard. They require hard work to survive. So many times I have found myself turning to those who know me best, since before I met my husband. Time and time again, I seek advice, solace, reflection, and validation in those relationships with my girlfriends. I strongly recommend keeping close to your best friends because when in troubled relationship waters, these gals know how to get you over the storm surges. Sometimes it's just a shared laugh that helps calm your nerves.

Here is a simple truth: your husband can be amazing in every way, and I hope for you that he is, but, please be clear—he is *not* your best girlfriend. Best girlfriends, as a group, are of a different nature entirely. The two are apples and oranges. They do not compare. Your husband may truly amaze you, but he does not want to ever *be* your best girlfriend. So don't expect him to relate to you the way she does; don't expect him to walk in her shoes. In expecting such of him, you only intentionally and willfully set yourself up for disappointment. And I think this single wrong move in relating to our partners sets us up for constant disappointment and anger toward men in general.

So what do I mean by this, and why is this conclusion even of importance? Simply put, in my opinion, confuse the nature of the two—your guy and your best girlfriend—

and you will fail to truly enjoy either. We must be honest with ourselves: we are wired (or conditioned, whichever one you prefer) to think we marry our best friend. In our late teens, our best friends are typically girls who hang on our every word, stay up listening to all our random and serious thoughts, and then share all their great nuggets of love and friendship in return. We talk and talk and talk with these best friends. In this we feel heard, validated, recognized, and cherished. And that is what makes a best friend.

So, a bit later on…we find a guy who amazes us and we flip for him and we talk and talk and talk…and then he gets *bored*. Honest, he gets bored and his eyes glaze over and he watches the TV or picks out his new car while driving and we just keep talking. And likely at some point, we notice. We see his lack of attention, his impatience while waiting for the conversation to end, or his random interruption with a completely unrelated topic. We ask, why? Why is he not listening? He used to listen. What changed? And there starts the doubt.

The bottom line is this…it does not matter *why* it changed. I suggest we all let that go. The important information is this: it *has* changed. He is now tired of listening to us verbalize our feelings. Trust me; he will escape to any safe place he can find just to get out of the never-ending "feelings" talk. And there starts the divide and the disconnect.

We are supposed to live happily ever after; he is supposed to be our "everything," our best friend. You marry your best friend…right? He will complete you. He is the "one." The truth is, no, he is not your "everything," he does not complete you, he is not your best girlfriend. And, it is not fair to expect him to be. That is a myth.

The problem lies often in this, it seems to me: the thrill of the early days. We meet our guy and we get completely consumed with spending all our time with him...getting to know each other. And it feels great. We are filled to the brim with the energy of connecting. It's amazing and we can't get enough. Our best girlfriend of yesteryear becomes a relationship we seem to invest in with less vigor. Sure, we still talk, but not the way we once did. And the relationship with the girls takes on a different tone. It's *girls night* now; we kick up our heels and run wild a bit. Maybe we don't really engage in those authentic talks the way we once did. But our friend understands, and maybe even has a new male energy all her own to enjoy. Everyone is cool...for now.

Anyone in a lengthy relationship will tell you, things change...the younger our age, it seems, the quicker they change...and we notice the change when our partner's eyes glaze over. He's not so enthralled with talking about the details, the blow-by-blow of your work world, or the family drama that seems to never end, or how angry you are at so-and-so for that ugly something he said. How could your partner be so cruel, how could he not *care*? And you doubt him now, because you expected him to not get *bored*. To him, all this talk is the same as yesterday's...and he just wants you to fix the situation. He does not want to talk about it more than once. In his world, there is no real sense in hashing this out again—just fix whatever is bothering you and move on. That is his nature. But your best friend of yesteryear is wired completely differently, hanging on your every word, though maybe she has heard it all a million times. Your best girlfriend has this nature. And we need that…that connection that inspires us with patience to let it out and feel heard.

So, if you invest all your energy in your guy, where do you turn when he is frustrated with listening? He still cares, but sees no purpose in talking about the same issues yet again. But you need to get this out…where do you go? Crazy. You go crazy if your best girlfriend is left back in yesteryear. You do. You go insane feeling unloved, unfulfilled, and alone. And then you get angry. Anger thrives in the destructive world. It tears things down, not builds them up. You are disappointed in your partner for not living up to your expectations—these expectations you set for him that completely disregarded his authentic nature. These are not fair expectations. He likely cannot live up to them, no matter how hard he tries.

We cannot let this happen. We must remember that much of our emotional needs as women can best be satisfied with an empathetic ear, often provided by the support of authentic relationships with women. Authentic relationships require honesty and respect. Invest in relationships with women whom you respect and admire. The greatest gift is to maintain a relationship based in authenticity with women who have known you since yesteryear. They've lived, laughed, and grown with you. They know you. This can't be done if you relegate those relationships to the time left over when maybe your guy is not around or busy with some other endeavor. I suggest you balance the time and make time for your girlfriends.

It is my strong belief that the happiest and most

fulfilled of women are those that find a balance in their connections with both men and women. I'll take it one step further: it is my belief that women who are in a committed relationship with a man must have strong connections to female friends. I think this is essential to being fulfilled. Because he is not your best girlfriend and he does not want to walk in her shoes. Expecting him to do so will most certainly lead to disappointment and anger. I ask you to invest in your investments equally, with both your guy and your girlfriends. Yes, the idea may be to spend the rest of your life with him; some of us still believe in that. But, I tell you this sincerely, you will not be spending the rest of your life with him happily if you try to set out solo, without the love and support of those great girlfriends of yesteryear. Invest in your relationships wisely.

Navigating the Waters of Change

"It develops a sense of equanimity; it opens you up to grace. Grace to me means the ability to hold the space of compassion for oneself and acceptance of life as it unfolds."

by Susan Halle

Susan Halle is a life coach, yoga teacher, and personal wellness consultant based in Montreal, Canada. She creates workshops that encourage community, wellness, and personal growth in both private and corporate settings. She is particularly passionate about working with women, as she believes in the power we hold as agents of change. She can be reached at www.blissworks.ca.

It is said that the only thing that is consistent in life is change. Certainly the aging process brings about changes that are obvious. At 30, we aren't the same person that we were at 16, nor do we expect to be the same when we hit 50. We can see changes in our minds, our bodies, and even our spiritual outlook. Most of these things come as expected, and we can look forward to maturing and growing.

Change can also come unexpectedly and throw us a curve that we had not anticipated in our wildest dreams.

We may have a vision of how we see our lives unfold. It may be the dream of a successful career, a loving partner, a family, a large home, or all of the above. We do the work, we set the course, with intention and optimism. And then the unthinkable occurs and the house of cards falls. What do we do then?

I speak of this because it happened to me. It has been a great gift, but at the time it was anything but. I share this story to offer the wisdom that can be received from a major life change, and to honor the stories that make up our lives.

When I was just 22, I set out on my own as a freelance graphic designer. Within a short time, I met the man who would become my husband and he joined me in building a successful corporate communications business, serving the financial industry. We traveled the world, bought anything our hearts desired, and life was great. We also spent a good deal of time in the gym, and were looking pretty buff and beautiful!

My husband met a personal trainer who sold him on the idea of anabolic steroids, and soon, without my knowledge, he was taking them regularly. Within a few months, the drugs set off a series of strange behaviors, which led first to infidelity and eventually to a physiological meltdown. Though we separated, we tried to work things out, but our business began to fail and tragically, my husband, having by that time become addicted to all sorts of prescription drugs as well, died of an overdose.

To say I was ill prepared for such an occurrence would be an understatement. However, I had developed some tools to cope with change well in advance of the chaos that had become my life in the years leading to his death. Not only did they carry me through, they led to a career change and to the path of helping others.

One of the great gifts I discovered was meditation. A great deal has been written about the effects of meditation lately. A meditation practice can really help you in times of trouble. It develops a sense of equanimity; it opens you up to grace. Grace to me means the ability to hold the space of compassion for oneself and acceptance of life as it unfolds. While sitting in meditation, one can experience just how busy the mind is. We learn to observe this busyness and allow it to unfold without getting caught up in it. And with that brings a sense of peace that is always accessible, no matter the situation.

Learning meditation is really as easy as watching your breath. There are many programs out there; some combine yoga, some are based in religion such as Christian or Buddhist meditations, and some are geared for pain and stress reduction. Finding what is most appropriate for you is essential, but even more important is just doing it! Following on that is the knowing that you are doing it right… Your mind will always be busy, but don't worry about it, just keep at it and watch some of the busyness quiet down…even for a split second!

For me, finding that very simple practice was a godsend. I was able to maintain calm in the face of all the changes that were to come. And there were many.

The face of business was changing as the late 1990s approached, and that, combined with a growing awareness of ecology, led me on my current career path. I began to consider whether what I was doing for a living was really what I was passionate about. And after a time and a fair bit of training, I became a personal trainer, yoga teacher, and life coach. What a joy it has been to help people reach their goals of a happier, healthier life!

Yoga can teach us many things other than postures and breathing. The foundations, the Yamas and Niyamas, help us to realize the important things in life. Truthfulness (*satya*), non-greediness (*aparigraha*), and contentment (*santosha*) are but a few of the principles from yoga that we take "off the mat." Learning the deeper practices of yoga can benefit us when in the change process. Yoga does not require us to change our religious views; it simply lets us become more connected with life itself.

The most beautiful part of a yoga practice or class is the end, *savasana*. In *savasana*, which is translated as "corpse pose," we learn to let go. Letting go of outcomes, of ideas, of beliefs and values that no longer serve us, is the cornerstone of moving through change with grace. Ultimately, we will need to let go of everything we believe we hold so dear, so we may as well practice now! By letting go, we make space for new beginnings. When we roll over after *savasana* and into a fetal position, we can use the metaphor for our own rebirth.

Taking care of our bodies is another essential part of navigating change. While it's easy to self-medicate with alcohol, food, and prescription drugs, we all know that this leads us down a slippery slope. Our health is one of the most precious gifts we have, and it is imperative to take care of it, especially when we are in stressful situations. Stress is one of the leading causes of illness, and abusing our health adds to health issues exponentially. If change has knocked on your door, send it all the kindness you can, with exercise, healthy unprocessed foods, plenty of rest, and good clean water. And if the change you are dealing with is an actual health problem, seek out alternative advice *as well as* allopathic medicine. Miracles have been known to happen with the many avenues of healing available to us today.

We are living in interesting times. There are countless books, articles, and messages being put out right now that lead many of us to believe that we are heading into chaotic and change-filled times. Whatever you may believe, it's a good idea to begin to inform yourself of some of the scientific truths of our age. The planet is getting warmer; the ice caps are melting, all of which is leading to changing weather patterns and possible ecological disasters. We are rapidly reaching peak oil, where we need to find alternative energy sources. As we face more global health epidemics, our food sources are in question and our way of life in the West quite simply is going to have to change.

I grew up as a tail-ender of the baby boom generation; the world was our oyster! In the past 50 years, this generation has been responsible for incredible inventions, but we have also consumed resources like no other generation before us. Many of us are looking at our children and saying, hey, wait a minute... Yes we have had it all, but we are paying a steep price, and we need you to lead the way now, into an era of balance and peace.

We all have a responsibility to become agents of change in this new world. We can examine our values and beliefs in the face of this emerging world. The shamans of South

America say we dream our world into reality and in order to change our world, we need to dream a new dream. How about dreaming a more peaceful existence, one where we can celebrate our similarities instead of our differences? How about the dream of every person on this planet having enough clean water, food, and access to health care, even if it means we will have to give up the idea that we will live in a large house with a luxury car? How about getting out into nature instead of trips to the mall for entertainment?

Using the same principles I have laid out for personal change management, we can allow emerging change to come with grace instead of chaos. We don't want a Hollywood disaster scenario, and I believe we don't need to have one. But we must begin now. Find your personal mission through meditation and self-inquiry. Look at your current values and compare them to the way you are living your life. Find a like-minded community and spread the seeds through social network sites and group gatherings. This does not have to be hippie-dippie! Look for simplicity and kindness. It's what the world needs today.

The only thing consistent in life is change, and the only way we can change the world is to change ourselves. I wish every one of us a life filled with the joy of change. Blessings!

Going the Distance

"The choices you make will not only impact your direction but also create additional challenges for those who find themselves at the crossing with you. "
by Barbara McMahon

For the last 20 years, Barbara Mintzer-McMahon has been working as an organizational consultant, executive coach, and trainer. She specializes in leadership development, team building, change management, and building strategic partnerships. In 1989 she founded The Center for Transitional Management (CTM) in Orinda, California. Barbara is also on the executive leadership team for The Alexcel Group and is currently the head of their Women in Leadership Consulting Division. For the last five years, she has been the senior lead of the coaching faculty for the Global Institute for Leadership Development. She facilitates workshops and consults both nationally and internationally for a wide variety of professional organizations including those in business, finance, media, high-risk occupations, hospitality, and education. She has keynoted and developed training programs for Women in Leadership, Strategic Partnering and Strategies for Successful Leadership for companies including Shell International, Intel, Pella Corporation, Nektar Therapeutics, and many others. She is available for coaching/consulting, keynotes, and trainings. To contact her, email thectm@aol.com

In my lifetime, I have participated in two kinds of endurance events: the ones that I voluntarily signed up for and the ones chosen for me by some larger power. They have both taught me great lessons about how to survive and thrive, as well as how to create sustainable transformational change.

Of these two options, I like the endurance events that I actually sign up for better. Personally, I appreciate the element of choice. These are the events where I am in charge of choosing what and when, such as signing up for my first marathon. I chose to do this when I was 49 years old and had an accumulated 10 years of experience in managing a sustained running program. This meant that I entered phase two, actually training for the marathon, with a fair amount of experience and understanding of what would be required and how these practices would impact my experiences.

This is not the case with the second type of endurance event, the unplanned and unexplained. These are the events that strike without warning and take you completely by surprise. The ones for which you have no previous training, no personal knowledge, and absolutely no real sense of how it will affect you and the life of which you are a part.

The two experiences are vastly different from one another, but both of them have taught me great lessons in what will be required to endure these stretch assignments and get to higher ground and a better life.

What I am personally committed to here is sharing my

stories and what I have learned along the way. My hope is that it will be of some support to you—food for thought, as you reflect on what is important in your journeying. What is happening in your life that is testing your endurance, requiring you to stretch? And, how might you face these challenges in a way that will help you to strengthen your core and bring you to higher ground?

Let me start by expanding a little more about the differences between these two types of events. The marathon, the planned event, was an experience I entered with a fair amount of confidence and positive anticipation. Although the journey to the event had been long, I had picked the place, created the vision of the experience and how I wanted to be within that vision (fit/confident), and had full control over the approach. It was an experience I had built up to. I had been researching, training, and gathering resources and support for over a decade. Although I could not know every detail about how the actual event would unfold or what to expect on that day, I had done my due diligence and felt prepared and fairly confident that whatever my experience, I would be better for it and would not endanger myself or anyone else I ran with along the way. This was not the case with my other set of experiences—managing the unexpected and unwanted.

The series of storms began in early 2007 when my husband was diagnosed with cancer. Just two weeks after this, my stepson was killed in a motorcycle accident and on the same night as his death, we found out that in about seven and a half months, we would be grandparents. This was definitely a time when life hit me backside of the head and knocked me into territory I had never been in before.

I found myself struggling to move and very frightened for my own survival, as well as the survival of those who were nearest and dearest to me.

What I know for sure is that in each of these types of experiences, one is brought to a crossing. It is a complicated place. Things are moving in every direction. The choices you make will not only impact your direction but also create additional challenges for those who find themselves at the crossing with you.

This is a place where there is a convergence of moving parts, each of which can have profound impact on the others. Over time, I have come to separate these parts into four major components. I now call them the 4P's of Transformational Change: Perception, Practices, Partnerships, and Performance. Let's explore each of these and the influence that mastering each can have on one's ability to go long distances or to achieve real and sustainable transformational change.

Perception: These are your beliefs, the way you think. Perception includes the way you see yourself, the way you see others, and the way you see and understand the situation or system you are in. On the flip side, it includes how the beliefs others hold impact the way they think, the ideas they hold about themselves, the way they see you, and the way they see the situation or system of which you are a part. These two sides are sometimes similar and sometimes not. However, they always influence each other.

Practices: This is all about what you do. Practices include the actions you take, the patterns you form, and the competencies or skill sets on which you choose to focus.

Partnerships: This is the dynamic way you interact with others and—perhaps even more important—the way you teach others to interact with you.

Performance: This area is about the vision you hold and the outcome you create.

At the Crossroads: Lessons that Endure

Whether preparing for the marathon or surviving through horrendous personal storms, what I realized was that if I was going to survive/thrive through these experiences, I needed to take the time to identify what I really valued most. I learned that anchoring into these values would make a critical difference to the choices I made and the future I created for myself. For example, because I valued my long-term health, I would not use performance-enhancing drugs to prepare for the race. Being successful at anchoring in this way can often be difficult, especially when what we believe about ourselves or the circumstances we are in obstructs us from anchoring into the values we hold.

Never had this held more truth for me than at the intersection of life events involving my husband's illness, the loss of our son, and the impending birth of our grandchild. The edge that we stood on was razor sharp. We had been cut to the core by losing Nate. We had two children that needed their father and me now more than ever. We also had a grandchild on the way.

My husband got very clear that what he focused on, the perceptions he held, would either give him strength beyond his limits or suck every breath of life out of him. It was also crystal clear that what thoughts/beliefs got shared with our two children and how we made sense and order of what was happening could profoundly influence not only each of us but our children and what they thought. It would influence the decisions they made and the actions (Practices) in which they engaged. Would they give up? Would they be able to focus on riding the wave on the strength of our love? We realized that the way we thought and communicated our beliefs to our children would have profound effect on what they perceived about themselves, about the values we held in family and the vision we promoted for the future. It was all connected.

I realized that how I traversed at this crossroad was critical. I had to drill down on every decision that I was making and ask myself:

What if? What if I choose to give up…then what? What would it mean for me? What would it mean for my partner or my children, for my clients, for all the people in my circle of influence? What impact would these actions have on my future and on theirs? It was only by going through this exercise and questioning the impact of directions/ actions I could take that I could truly get control back in my life.

It also helped to ask myself if I could stand in front of my significant others and communicate these choices to them. Could I reveal what I had uncovered? This was key in helping me to know if this was a truly viable path. Would it create the kind of change I wanted? What would it take for me and for others to manage this course, to survive, and to thrive through these most challenging of times?

I am 57 now. What I have learned through preparing

for the planned events and surviving the unexpected tests of endurance is that there is no single fail-safe set of answers. I have developed a clarity about how important it is, during periods of extreme challenge, to practice the interval method. I have learned to move from periods of intense inquiry to action, and then return to inquiry and then back to action.

So in closing, I will leave you with eight critical questions I have found key to managing at the crossroads. And, I wish you the best of journeys.

Eight Critical Questions to Remember

1. What is the vision I hold? Where do I want to take myself and others?
2. What if I get there? What will that mean for me, for my partners, and the system of which we are a part?
3. What decisions do I want to make about that?
4. Am I able/willing to communicate my choices to others?
5. How do my perceptions/beliefs about myself, the situation, and others support or obstruct the intended outcome (performance)? How am I impacted by the beliefs others have of me?
6. Are my beliefs enabling me to anchor into my values?
7. What are the practices/actions I need to eliminate/enhance to support my partnerships, my values, my vision, and myself?
8. If not now, when?

Your Heart—The Key to Unlocking Your Gift Box

"As I slowly uncover my talents that came in this wrapped-up present that was given me at birth, and as I draw on these talents the way my heart tells me to, I thrive."

by Joanne Chan

Joanne Chan, a Chinese American now living in Asia, is a molecular biologist, a marketing executive, and an advocate for neglected children. Besides her love for cooking and sports, her passion is to see pharmacogenomics becoming reality, and to alleviate children's suffering. She regularly speaks in workshops for work and for her church and can be contacted by email: joannepchan@gmail.com.

I will never forget the look on their faces as these children opened the gift package. It was a look of overflowing joy and deep gratitude. These gift packages are simply school bags stuffed with goodies, from toys to towels to treats. They were brought over by our team who went to Uganda this past summer and were given to each of the HIV-positive children in an orphanage there. As they took out each item, they responded with new excitement, and they would either play with the item or eat it. Though I must say, the excitement subsided a bit as soon as they popped the durian candy into their mouth. You can tell Asians packed these gifts.

I once read in a book that each of us comes with a package when we are born. In this package are our gifts and talents, and it is by following our hearts that we discover them and use them for our ultimate fulfillment. It is our responsibility to unfold this package and use everything that is bestowed upon us. I had only a faint idea of what my passions were; they were somewhere along the line of healthcare, helping underprivileged children, molecular biology, serving people, and culinary art. But I had also heard so many people tell me that as long as I found a job that I did not hate, I should consider myself blessed. I was glad that my idealistic self refused to believe it. I proved myself right when I took the first step of faith to follow my heart and saw the beauty of the truth.

As I was working as a molecular biologist, I was excited to apply most of what I'd learned at the university. During my five years as a scientist I loved being engrossed in science and developed my critical thinking. However, I came to realize that what I actually enjoyed most was the rare chance to present my project to the department. I would get so energized whenever I was up there explaining scientific concepts to a big audience. The slight problem was, I came across opportunities like that only once a year, twice at the most. Besides talking in front of a big group I also love to meet people, which is something I felt I did not do enough as a scientist. I also did not feel my work was directly impacting the people I was most concerned with:

the underprivileged, abandoned, suffering children.

That was when I was 26 and having a great life. I enjoyed the comfort and fun as a young professional. Yet a voice in my heart kept reminding me of the other passions that I'd conveniently ignored. I had always wanted to work in an orphanage in a third-world country, but it seemed more like a dream that an achievable task. Until one day the voice in my heart was yelling so loud that I had to do something about it. To everyone's surprise, I decided to quit my comfortable job to volunteer in South Africa for five months, with no clear idea of what I would do after this volunteering trip. I managed to reduce the possessions in my apartment to fit in two suitcases, and off I went to volunteer to in a rural village called Heidelberg and serve as a primary school teacher, as well as in an orphanage in Knysna as a caretaker. I thought I was making a sacrifice by going, but what I gained in return was incredible. I was surrounded by the children's abundant love during the few months I was there. During that time I learned so much about myself, including both weaknesses and strengths, and I discovered more of what had been stored in this "package" that was given me. I confirmed my love and passion for helping marginalized children, but at the same time I found out I am not cut out to be a caretaker. There are people out there who are simply more apt to be caregivers, and my gifts are different. I was not discouraged by this truth. I might not be fit to be a full-time caretaker, but I am fit to love these underprivileged children. My heart tells me to keep looking for ways to serve them, and I continue to follow it.

After my trip to South Africa, I went to Hong Kong to

visit my parents. What was meant to be a quick visit lasted almost three years. Just one week after I landed in Hong Kong, my father was admitted to the emergency room for chest pain. It turned out he was having an aortic dissection, a condition that is frequently fatal. But praise God, he beat the odds and survived the emergency surgery. During the two months he was in intensive care, my heart was loudly speaking to me again as I felt a strong urge to stay close to my father. *Who has loved you more than anything? What would truly bless him at this stage in his life?* I had never considered moving back to Hong Kong, but at that point it was no longer about me. My desire to be closer to my father was so immense that I let go of what I wanted at the moment. So I sold my car, bid farewell to my friends, and embarked on a journey with a mission to encourage my father.

I took the first job that was offered to me, as a salesperson for a pharmaceutical company. It was hell. It did not fit my personality at all, and I had a hard time adjusting to life in Hong Kong. But after a mere three months, in the most peculiar way, I received a call from the HR manager of my current company and was invited for an interview for a marketing position in its healthcare department. Though I had no prior marketing experience, I was offered a position with the regional marketing team, looking after molecular diagnostics products for Asia. My molecular biology background proved helpful for the position and I was able to continue pursuing my passion for science, and especially for molecular biology. I had to travel more than 50 percent of the time, but instead of finding it tiring, I would get energized by it and I loved the exposure to different cultures. As my product helps doctors to monitor patients who are infected with HIV, I learned and talked a lot about HIV in my job. I also got to learn that there are many children who are infected with this lethal virus by their parents at birth. But the good news is, with good nutrition and the right treatment, these children can live for 20 to 30 years!

My heart reminded me again of the marginalized children that need to be cared for. Buried in the busyness of this job, I realized I had not done enough to love the kids who are most neglected and ignored. I wrestled with the inability to fulfill my passion for these children with my job. Then one day in my church, an announcement about a mission trip to Uganda caught my attention. They were looking for volunteers to go and build a classroom for orphans. The thought of going kept lingering in my mind until again I could no longer fight the voice of my heart. So I stepped out in faith to go to this unfamiliar place, to find myself being rewarded tremendously. My eyes were opened to see the simple joy and hope in the abandoned and neglected children in Africa. The trip was so meaningful that I felt this was something I wanted to do again. Not long after I came back, I was asked to consider leading the trip the following year. I was told that we would build a classroom for another orphanage, which cares only for children who are HIV-positive. My heart was stirred. It did not take long before I committed to the church that I would co-lead this trip. Every single minute of planning the trip was nothing but enjoyment, and I devoted my whole heart to it. I looked forward to all the meetings, and I was passionate about sharing my vision to the team. I had never felt so alive. In the end we had 35 people on the team, and we all had high expectations for this trip and wanted it to be a life-changing experience. We went in the summer of 2009 and we all came back changed. There were precious lessons of humility, love, and hope. We saw the overflowing joy and the unceasing hope of the children. They truly live from their hearts: they live to give, to reach out, and to love.

If you asked me four years ago I would never imagine coming to Asia, and doing what excites me every single day. But here I am. I am in a place where my gifts and my passions harmonize, and I am living them now because I heard and acted on the small, still voice from my heart. So many voices whisper to us every day, telling us to settle, to stay in our comfort zone, or that going after what we believe in is too much of a hassle. What I came to find is that there is no other way to live a fulfilling life but to pay attention to what your heart tells you and live in accordance to your passion. As I slowly uncover my talents that came in this wrapped-up present that was given me at birth, and as I draw on these talents the way my heart tells me to, I thrive. I thrive not to be recognized; I thrive so that I am more and more prepared to carry out what I am created to do. And when every fiber of my body is energized and synchronized with each other to connect with my passion, I am genuinely fulfilled. I walk and breathe and work with the absolute joy of knowing I have a purpose and am accomplishing it. Anyone can have this joy. Just follow your heart.

It Takes a Village...

"Things would come to me when I least expected it, and I would process and express these feelings and leave them somewhere out there on the roadway."

by Desi Klaar

Desi Klaar holds a master's degree in Human Resource Management and is currently pursuing a doctoral degree in Organizational Development. She believes in enhancing employee retention, development, and organizational fiduciary responsibility in upper education, while managing a compensation and benefits department. A member of various health and welfare councils that support disease prevention and healthy living, Desi has been instrumental in providing wellness programs for a trust in the San Diego area.

Never be bullied into silence. Never allow yourself to be made a victim. Accept no one's definition of your life, but define yourself.—Harvey S. Firestone

After years of counseling in secrecy and still feeling valueless, unappreciated as a productive member of society, somehow different from others who led a more charmed life...one afternoon while riding 100 miles through a Southern California desert on my bicycle I had an epiphany.

I elect to be a victim…

The Past

I realize looking back that before my family unit fell apart and then became two different, unruly family units with the pageantry of failed relationships and divorces throughout the years on both sides, prior to that, I was the central focus of my family's attention. I was told that I was special, that I was a worthy part of a secure family unit. As an adolescent, I was excused by my parents as they were preoccupied by their personal relationship dysfunctions. As time went on and I entered high school, I noticed that I was no longer regarded as unique and the center of attention, anywhere. I was herded through the halls and prepared for college with the other kids in my class. Both at home and at school, I was told to fend for myself and grow up. This exposure was more than I could digest. No nurturing or preparation was given, unless I visited a friend's house and sought out what I was lacking.

I adopted a personal preservation tactic that carried me into young adulthood. If I cannot depend on the structure around me, then I am going to "the village" for advice and direction. The long-term effect of this life choice is that choosing to isolate relatives only widens the hemorrhaging dysfunction of the already strained family unit. Even today, members of my family are still in a continuous state of unrest. I have become the rock, the one stable family unit member, whereas decades ago, I was considered a runaway and noncommittal; my reactionary responses to family turmoil left my future looking bleak.

This family turmoil gave me a sense of constant alertness

and anxiety; I remained light on my feet, in case the ground below me began to shift again. Afraid to commit to future plans as they might be cancelled or forgotten given our family dynamics, I would not look past the next weekend. Simple tasks such as paying rent were hard to plan for in my early adulthood, as I'd never learned these basic skills.

Rejection, fear, shame, anger, and perceived injustices by family members led to my deciding to lead my own life and not commit to anyone or anything. I placed my fate on the wind and rode the wave. No one warned me that postponing responsibility and planning for the future would in time become an issue. I would not have listened even if the warning had come. I trusted no one's opinion and always thought that my way was best.

While the village was raising me in my late teens and early twenties, I seemed to begin heeding the advice of random people who had what I wanted. Slowly my future began to become a goal. Baby steps toward commitment and security were becoming more comfortable each year. Not only did I want to achieve a goal, but I finally felt deserving of my achievements.

While playing catch-up as a young adult, I realized that I'd reached a commitment and responsibility quandary. I wanted what my parents had, but did not want to begin that sacrificial lifestyle that I watched them toil over year after year. I was stuck with early-20s values and was graduating into adult desires. Once again, I had to go to the village and ask how to bridge the gap between what I wanted and where I was. My advisors all stated that I needed to go back to school and finish my degree. I needed to become marketable, to hone my presentation and delivery. Stop verbalizing in trendy speak; revamp the résumé and buy conservative business attire. Costume jewelry and personal issues did not belong in the workplace. The best advice ever was to turn off my home life when I stepped into the office. This information would serve me well on my career interviewing path. After a few practice interviews, I secured my first professional position, which allowed me to begin building the bridge to my new future.

Getting Past the Past

Don't become a victim of yourself. Forget about the thief waiting in the alley; what about the thief in your mind? — Jim Rohn

Getting over "me" was a long and painful process. The self-destructive behavior that I continually stumbled through shadowed the patchwork of success that I allowed myself to feel good about. My shame and insecurity was so prevalent that a casual compliment from someone would immediately invoke a negative comment back, negating that person's verbal gift to me. At times I would outwardly react with anger, shutting out the complimenting person. Realizing that I was being destructive and desiring true friendship and acceptance, I would have to apologize and announce my deficiencies on the spot. I took on a new approach to my own negativity. If I had to continually admit to others that I was working on my defects of character, I was hoping that I would become aware of my reactionary behavior. That I would someday become sick and tired of hearing myself apologize for being continually negative.

I knew that nothing in my life would change until I

changed something. Becoming less reactionary and more proficient in kindergarten basics was so difficult. I was told by a very wise villager that I needed to fake it until I made it. I faked it until I had become close to a few co-workers who were used to my continual apologetic practice. Sometimes they would grin if I was taking a negative approach to something. I noticed that I was beginning to make connections and trust others as being genuinely interested in me, as I was in them.

My second approach to becoming less reactionary and more proactive in my human interaction skills was to begin asking others, "How can I help?" Let me tell you, I really had no desire to help others with their work or personal issues…I thought they should be helping me…I was the busiest in the office. I would be wishing as I was asking the question, "Please say that you do not need my help." At first, I am sure that my tone and facial expressions assisted them in saying that they did not need my assistance. As time went on, I realized that I was softening my tone, and I was then involved in all sorts of committees, projects, and volunteer positions. Amazing how much I learned about their workload and how minimal mine really was…

My Presence

Learning how to communicate and empathize with others sparked an interest in continuing my education and pursuing my master's degree. Oddly enough, my newfound passion was in the human resources field. I was so interested in hearing about laws that protect employees that I maneuvered my career over the next few years to assist and support the mission statements of multiple nonprofit organizations and school districts. The self-realization that was sparking in me was feeding my fire to assist those who were seeking a confidant who would protect their rights. Twenty-five years ago, I would never have imagined that I would pursue a career in human resource management.

Keeping with my village theory, one of my new office friends suggested that I run a marathon. At the time, I was significantly overweight and hadn't run a mile since I was in my teens. While training, I met a few runners who took me under their wing and taught me everything I needed to know, and I ran that marathon. The bond that I created with this new village of runners was priceless… they were so giving and patient. I finally had a hobby that was mine…my own individual accomplishment. But most importantly, I had an outlet that allowed me private time to think while running or cycling alone. Time to get past the past and process what still lingered. Things would come to me when I least expected it, and I would process and express these feelings and leave them somewhere out there on the roadway. I loved this time alone; this time to be all right with myself; this time to reflect on the blessings that I had been experiencing in recent years. Within the next five years I completed a handful of marathons, ultra-marathon races, and Ironman triathlons.

Since finishing my master's degree, competing in various endurance races, and building welcoming relationships both professionally and personally, I have created long-lasting worldwide connections. I communicate with people each month on multiple continents. Our relationships are strong and supportive. These connections are continuing my "it takes a village" theory. I depend on their support and accountability to assist me in my continuing growth and perseverance. To know that I can travel just about anywhere and meet up with someone for a cup of coffee or a long run is very comforting.

The villagers are never far from my mind. Looking back, I am sure that my self-preservation techniques were drastic and seemed defiant to those who were closest to me in my family. Decades later, it is all water under the bridge, and I have explained my youthful wanderings to everyone. I took the path less traveled and have become sensitive to those around me. I have a clear understanding of others who are seeking positive growth and improvement in their life. I have empathy for those who are victims, whether they know they feel that way or not. I have found what works for me, what allows me to be the wise and confident woman that I have evolved into. I am finally a villager who is assisting those who seek friendship, direction, and advice. My travels have groomed me to become a professional with vision and insight in situations that occur in my personal life and in the human resources industry.

Living from the Heart

"Our lives can always be filled with "if only," so I try to
listen to myself and be true to how I'm feeling."
By Diana Brandt
President of Azure Hollywood Productions

*We are all born with certain gifts, yes, God-given gifts.
There was a five-year-old girl named Diana who could paint
and draw details beyond the ordinary stick figure. She could
illustrate pictures with real people, animals, plants, and trees
along with a cottage, a brook, and a footbridge. She was also
very expressive during music and dance periods. She loved the
film Mary Poppins and had her mother and grandmother
take her to see it at least five times. The part she enjoyed the
most was the idea of being able to walk into a sidewalk chalk
drawing.*

Diana's mother, a single parent, had enrolled in a
formal Fine Arts program at USC and discovered that
making a living as an artist wasn't an easy thing to do, so
she advised her daughter not to waste her time with art.
The message Diana received at a very early age was that art
wasn't practical and that she should focus on doing well
in academic subjects such as math, science, history, and

English. So she let go of her innate gift in art. Instead, she struggled in academic subjects such as math, where she had no gifts at all. She was a very good student, however, so she went on to college, graduating from UCLA in Political Science (Pre-Law) in 1984. All this was primarily done to please her parents and grandparents, but not Diana. She entertained the idea of going on to law school until she discovered through numerous interviews with attorneys that it wasn't going to be the right fit for her temperament and personality. She needed to be in a field that allowed room for creativity and expression. Her journey to discover what was best for her has been long, only to find out later in her life that she is an artist, a born artist.

Why share this with you? Our lives can be better clarified if we can get the right direction and support at an early age. My mother, who did introduce me to art, and father insisted on a formal academic education. Unfortunately, instead of helping me to flourish, their direction derailed me. I've spent my life primarily off track, trying to figure out what's missing so I could right myself. I still don't paint or work with my hands. During my journey, I've discovered parts of myself that I probably would never have discovered if I had been content with a specific career path. This discovery is that writing is an art form that allows one the ability to paint with words. It also allows great expression, so somehow I stumbled into learning this—the hard way, of course!

Our lives can always be filled with "if only," so I try to listen to myself and be true to how I'm feeling. The saying "be true to oneself" is lightly thrown around, but we really need to heed it. It can be difficult and a great challenge to follow through with our inner feelings and desires because we fall into the habit of pushing them down, subverting them, and ourselves for that matter, turning ourselves off in effect and losing the ability to really hear our own voices. With years of conditioning to listen to others' expectations and wishes for us, we become people-pleasers, and in most cases we simply become lost.

With a new perspective, I realize now that I must have been quite a challenge to my mother because I was a very determined, competitive, strong-willed child. For example, if my mother told me I was grounded and had to go to my room for back-talking her, I would simply say okay and then climb out of my bedroom window to join up with the rest of the neighborhood kids. I had a sense about what I needed to do, and I would do it!

On a lazy summer day, I would think, "Ahh, this is the perfect day to bake cookies and sell lemonade." Then I would begin baking in the kitchen and squeezing lemons into a pitcher. I would imagine how nice it would be to be a traveler and come upon a young girl not only with lemonade and cookies to sell, but also original pastel artwork that she was making as she sat. One day when I had my lemonade and cookie stand set up and began producing pastel drawings, a young man pulled up and got out of his car.

He walked around and viewed the spread and then began analyzing my pastel drawings. His glance settled on the bumblebee. He then asked me to draw him one, so I did. When I was finished, he gave me 10 cents and told me to watch the Saturday morning cartoons, because my bumblebee was going to be making a special appearance.

He told me he loved my drawings and that he worked for Disney Studios. My mother really couldn't keep up with all the things I was up to. That Saturday morning I told her to watch this cartoon. We watched together and sure enough my bumblebee made an appearance, a whole beehive full!

I had many successes as a child, but there was one that stood out above the rest. It began in my front yard, where I would stand observing the ants on the sidewalk. Mr. Therman would ride by on an old bike he'd fixed up with a basket and a bell on the front. He would wave and ring the bell as he rode by me. He was the neighborhood handyman, who seemed very old to me with his white-gray hair, but looking back I think he probably was only in his late 40s or early 50s. I would watch him as he turned into his driveway about two houses down from ours and then walk over to say "Hello," the usual greeting I'd give, plus this question: "Mr. Therman, are you going to be polishing rocks today?" If he answered yes, I'd immediately ask, "Can I watch?" I don't really remember a day where he turned me down. Once he would give me the okay, I'd follow him around as if we were playmates, even though he was much, much older.

Everything about what Mr. Therman would get up to intrigued and excited me. He was a man who liked to take action, work with his hands, and he also didn't mind getting a bit dirty, which made him cool. He had a rock collection under museum-quality glass cabinets throughout the living room and den areas of his home. In his backyard he created a magical garden, something you would expect to see at Disneyland. There were lavender, green, pink, red ... crystal balls, rocks of all shapes and sizes with different sides polished off to give one a view into their glistening, colorful patterns that were hidden. All this, along with a beautiful stream that pooled into a pond below with koi fish, tropical plants, and baby's tear grass, flourished on every inch of soil in his yard. On the side of his house he had built himself a workshop that was set up for cutting and polishing rocks. Mr. Therman was a retired geologist who remained a very happy rock hound in the San Fernando Valley.

I would sit on a stool next to him as he polished rocks in his workshop. He seemed to enjoy my company and my incessant questions, such as, "Why do you like polishing rocks?" He always gave me good answers, so we were friends. I noticed he would always discard a lot of rock debris that was mostly flat polished pieces. After my mother had taken me to the Los Angeles County Museum, where I had viewed hand-painted eggs, I got an idea. I asked my mother if it was hard to paint the eggs and how come they didn't rot. She told me they blew the egg yolks out. When we got home, she showed me how to do that by making needle holes on either side of the egg and blowing. Almost every day for a week I was blowing out egg yolks for eggs and collecting them, but was afraid to paint on them. I asked Mr. Therman if I could take some of the rock debris to use for a project I was working on, and he said okay.

Next, I enlisted my brother to help me in my assembly-line project, gluing individual eggs to a flat polished rock base. I left the eggs white but added color by placing dried flowers into them. Then I decided to ride my bike to our local Hallmark, where I'd noticed they had glass shelves in all the front windows with merchandise displayed there.

I asked the owner, "How do people get to sell their stuff in the store?" He asked me why I asked, so I showed him my decorative eggs. He then took them from me and placed them on a shelf in the front window and told me that he would sell them for $3.00, adding, "If people buy them you will make 50 percent of the sale, which means you'll get half the profit, $1.50." He explained that he kept the other half for renting his space in the store. This got me very keen to bring him more, because now I was in business. My decorative eggs sold, the price was raised to $5.00, and I continued to bring him at least 10 to 20 more every few weeks. Again, my mother had no clue about this experience until after the fact.

At nighttime, an hour before you go to bed, just rest your head on your pillow and think about yourself as a child. Can you visualize yourself at age three? Most people say that is the age where they consciously remember certain events or activities in their life. If you can't remember yourself then, try the next year up, age four. Once you settle on the age you can begin to remember yourself being, really begin to focus in on as much as you can remember during that age before you begin focusing on the next year. Most people come up with only two or three memories that stand out, so don't feel like your memory is failing you if you can't think of much more, just move on. Think about what pleased you, what made you happy, and what you considered your childhood successes even if others were cruel by not recognizing them as such. What counts here is how you felt about it!

I've Got Your Crazy

"Eventually the time came for me to go into the darkness,
to face my shadow so that I might reemerge as an
integrated whole."
By Giana Cicchelli

*Giana Cicchelli holds a master's degree in Sociology from
Cal State Fullerton (2010), and is both a high priestess in
the Wiccan tradition and a Pompamasayoq in the Peruvian
tradition. Giana has attended women's circles with many
goddess worshipers, met and worked with the new resurgence
of spiritual practitioners, attended Native American sweat
lodges (Lakota and non-Lakota), as well as traveled to both
the sacred valley and the jungles of Peru. She considers it is
both a privilege and an honor to do this work. She can be
contacted at www.gianacicchelli.com.*

In my mid-20s, I began to have a real interest in finding
my power. Too often I was involved in relationships that
drained me and left me feeling worthless. I decided that
I was going to strengthen my connection to spirit, and
no one could any longer tell me what I did not already
know. It was at the beginnings of this journey towards
self-actualization that I encountered what I now term the

"mirrored crazy," which is actually a double entendre.

My first steps were investigating and studying alternative forms of religious expression; any doctrine that I had believed due to my upbringing and socialization was out the window in favor of perspective expansion. I didn't realize how scary it could be to disown my foundation of beliefs, and with the same breath I began to feel very brave. Years before the beginnings of my spiritual journey I had been told by a psychic to look in the mirror for three minutes while saying, "I am the I am" (or at least that's how I remember it). When she told me this, I had a fear of looking in the mirror for anything longer than a glance. Something about the mirror scared me. It took me three years to decide it was time to face my fear, and just do it. I did. "I am the I am. I am the I am. I am the I am." After about a minute, I noticed a green shining light appear to draw itself around both of my eyes, and then loop up to what would be my third eye. I got so excited that, of course, it disappeared. I ran into the living room to tell my roommate.

"I saw my third eye!" I exclaimed.

"You're crazy!" my roommate replied, fully intending the meaning.

It was the beginning of a trend. Since that experience, I have noticed that whenever I made a realization, or experienced a revelation, there were always those who would wish to detract from my excitement. Detractors, and many times they were women! I was being a spiritual adventurer, charting off into the unknown, fully exploring my abilities and potential power, and my friends were telling me that I was crazy.

At first I was ashamed; I did not want to be considered crazy. I would go about my business no longer sharing my new experiences and understandings. There were a few friends that I could confide in, but otherwise I preferred to keep this new knowledge secret. A woman keeping her power secret, hmmmm, sounds familiar! I attended workshops, read books, and danced under the full moon. I fully interacted with the mystical teachings that were all around me, and grew stronger and stronger in my connection to spirit. I began to see that people around me who had abandoned their truths, abandoned their essence, and abandoned their dreams were the first to call me crazy. I began to notice this because my life was getting more full, fulfilling, intense, and colorful! I was becoming more myself, and happier with every day that passed.

Eventually the time came for me to go into the darkness, to face my shadow so that I might reemerge as an integrated whole. The shadow self is like looking in a mirror, the mirror I never let myself gaze into before, to see all of me, even the parts that are ugly. I was scared, but I knew that my teachings would guide me, and my connection to spirit would show me the way. Like the story of Hecate and Persephone, I needed only to follow the crone bearing torches to find my way out.

When I reemerged my knowledge was great, my experiences were ineffable, and my spirit was bright. My friends noticed the change instinctually and would respond with a newfound respect. It was in this moment that I no longer feared "my crazy" and began to be who I am. I painted pictures on my car, I danced around, I laughed, I howled at the full moon and played dress-up for fun. I am crazy!! I am full of crazy! It was allowing myself to become a little crazy that began the whole journey.

Now, as I continue this journey at the age of 30, I am still chided with "you're crazy" from acquaintances (though many fewer than before). I laugh and say, "That's why you love me!" But a new realization occurred to me about embracing my crazy: being crazy is a little bit scary to those who haven't embraced theirs. I am *craaaaaazy!* I do crazy things, and I don't care if people think I'm crazy. It is part of the power of being a woman! The power to create, the power to manifest, the power to birth from within myself new life; now, that is crazy! It is my position in society. Birth only comes from chaos. People only call it crazy if they are afraid to create themselves.

So, what am I telling women from the ages of 25 to 35? I am telling them that it is time to raise our heads, and our voices in unison, shouting "I got your crazy!" while dancing the rhythms of life with our hips and bursting forth with new vision. The world has been stagnating for a long, long time under the oppression of linear thinking and building monuments out of inflexible, unmovable cement. Our power is in our hips, our power is in our earthquakes, to bring down the monuments of antiquity that were audacious enough to think they could keep the creation down. Women are creation. We are the crazy energy that brings birth from death. Our connections to the unknowable mysteries have long been a source of jealousy for men. Not all men. Great men throughout time have looked to women for initiation into the great mysteries, and for their respect they were granted knowledge of the secrets. Today, many women have forgotten that they carry the secrets inside them, that they *deserve* to be revered and respected for the power they keep. But we have to claim our power, we have to claim our journey, charting into fear, and reemerging again.

We need to remember. Remember with me! Medusa was a priestess of Athena who was not made into an ugly old hag, but was granted the wisdom of snakes and the prestige of a sage. The goddesses are not mythos to be carried in our purses but living, breathing energy to be called upon in times of need, to be prayed to and given reverence. The great mystics throughout history knew that the women carried the secrets. Now, it is time for us to remember. When you look into the mirror, can you look for more than a glance? Do you accept what you see? Can you say, "I've got your crazy!"?

The Power of Peculiar, My Prescription
"I listen within mindfully and my intuitive intelligence
guides the way."
By: Rani Naik

*Rani is an advisor, author, and adventuress. She
authentically aligns people and startups with their powerful
passionate purpose and by guiding them to achieve excellence in
innovation. Rani is the founder of RaniRx Advisors and author
of RaniRx: The Power Prescription (TM) and The xFactor,
Excellence in Innovation. She advises and internationally
ignites innovation and excellence with the Power Prescription.
Rani can be reached at www.RaniRx.com.*

For most of my life I've been...well, different. I look
different, and feel different, from most people around me.

I was born and raised in California and Germany. My
parents are immigrants; my father is from Southern India,
my mother, Northern Germany. I grew up seeing the
world firsthand, as my father worked in travel and tourism.
My parents' friends joked that visiting our home was like
being at the UN. My mind has always been very open
and curious. I grew up speaking German, and as an adult
wanted to learn new languages and live in the countries I

had only explored as a tourist.

In my early twenties, after finishing my undergraduate degree in humanities with the desire to be well rounded and cultivating a mind that loves to learn, I went to work in Switzerland on an internship at Migros, the oldest and largest grocery chain in the country. There I was able to use my German language skills and live the culture and learn how the organization flowed, I was thrilled! This led me to live and work in such places as Australia, Brazil, and Germany, I found jobs in a range of fields as an English teacher, Headhunter, I trusted my gut and found interesting work wherever I went. Naturally, my love of people led me to explore psychology and spirituality, and how that intersects with business. This led to creating a system by which people and organizations can flourish to their fullest potential. In Brazil I studied with Shamans in the Amazon jungle on how to thrive in authenticity and achieve ones true potential. By working with the underlying spirit in all life; plants, humans, organizations and using this relationship and the power of singing and sound with natural knowing, I was able to refine and define the essential places where people and systems worked. I can clearly see the root causes of where and why they don't work and how to evolve this and bring about their highest potential.

However, my journey wasn't always a smooth one. Along the way, I met with a great deal of judgment from people. I would then try to fit in and fail...miserably and consistently. I wish someone had told me early on that failure is feedback - not an identity. This would have saved me much heartache.

Just as in the ugly duckling tale, it wasn't until I grew

into my signature swan that I could sing my own song with pride. Thus realizing that my uniqueness holds value and power in the world. I now have a presence and a purpose that is mine alone. My voice, my values—these are virtues, not vices. When I act with faith in myself, I flourish and feel great. When I give away my power, hoping to stay safe, small, and secure, I achieve failure.

I have a gift for clearly seeing the potential and challenges facing people and startups. This adds value, in a way no one else can, to people deciding to achieve their dreams. I have traveled to about fifty countries, where my love of life, culture, and learning flourishes to this day. Thereby, feeding my soul. Being fluent in three languages, everywhere I go it's easy to talk to people from around the globe and enjoy the satisfaction of being a world citizen.

By simply honoring my authentic alignments, I am satisfied! I listen within mindfully and my intuitive intelligence guides the way. I have come to realize that people may judge me regardless of what I do. Living in authentic alignment with my heart, I choose to love myself and now, love my life! The people around me value me, because I value myself. Today, I understand that we are all divinely designed to be who we are and do what we love. Peculiar is powerful!

Men Supporting Women In Sync

Become the Leader of Your Own Life

"If the "shoulds" in your life are coming from your own mind, make some time to examine them, one by one."
by Simon Vetter

Simon Vetter works with managers who want to create positive changes and professionals who want to create a STAND OUT brand. He is a business coach, speaker, and author, specializing in leadership effectiveness, behavioral change, and personal brand management.

Over the course of his career, he has coached, trained, and advised managers and teams from Agilent Technologies, CalPERS, Callaway Golf, Daimler, Johnson & Johnson, Microsoft, REMAX, Siemens, Toyota, US Steel, UBS, and other companies. His clients engage him because they want more clarity, focus, and personal balance. He assists them in improving behaviors, effectively influencing others, developing high-performing teams, and delivering results.

His latest book is STAND OUT! Branding Strategies for Business Professionals. He offers practical solutions on advancing one's career, finding personal fulfillment at work, and establishing a credible, attractive personal brand.

With 20 years of experience in marketing, sales, and leadership development, Simon combines an MBA-equivalent degree in Business and Marketing from the University of Bern. He is a member of Alexcel Group, a worldwide alliance of executive coaches; serves on the board of directors of the San Diego World Trade Center, and is a member of Toastmasters. Simon grew up in Switzerland and has lived in San Diego, California for 12 years. He speaks fluent English and German.

It was a gloomy Saturday morning in January when I first met Elaine, a classy lady in her mid-50s with a sharp mind and a way with people. The owner and founder of a high-end jewelry design company, Elaine started her business over 20 years ago, and her reputation in the industry spoke for itself. She was savvy and capable, but she had reached her limit.

She looked at me with frustration and despair, threw up her hands, and sighed, "I am just not having any fun anymore." She confessed that she felt desperate, unmotivated, and irritated with her own team. "To tell you the truth, I'd sell my business right now for one dollar."

It was a surprising thing to hear her say. In so many ways, she was living the dream—she had a successful business doing what she loves…except, as it turned out, these days she wasn't doing what she loved very much at all.

When I asked how she spent her workweek, she said, "In addition to designing, I manage the business, direct my team, negotiate with suppliers, and I travel over 100 days per year to sell my jewelry to retailers across the country."

This talented artist, an exceptionally creative and innovative woman, had followed her passion and built a great business. But her road to success was taking her farther and farther from her passion: designing jewelry.

With an understanding smile, I said, "No wonder you are exhausted. You do four different jobs: designing, selling, running the business, and managing your employees. What about delegating more to your team?"

"I would if I could, but I can't rely on them! They don't do the things I ask them to do, and I constantly have to check on them. I feel like I have to do everything." It was clear she had an uncommitted, underperforming team.

"Elaine, you're headed in the right direction with your business, but you're dragging a lot of dead weight on your team. You already know they are slowing you down, exhausting you, even...isn't it time to let them go?"

Watching her face closely, I saw a wave of discomfort come over her. Elaine was holding tightly to something that didn't work for her, a sure sign of an internal conflict. Her head knew she had a lousy team, but something inside was afraid to see them go.

Over the next few weeks, we uncovered some similarities between her ways of relating to the team and her childhood job of caring for her younger siblings. She had a strong belief that "I have to take care of others."

But her team didn't want to be "taken care of" or "bossed around." These managerial tactics made them feel resistant, uninspired, and even petulant. After all, if you treat people like children long enough, sooner or later they'll act accordingly.

The harder she pushed, the more they resisted. No

wonder they weren't having fun anymore. Everyone in her company was intensely focused on what they *didn't* like! And everyone felt powerless to change it.

In a situation like this, there's only one thing to do: get crystal clear on what you can change, and what you cannot. More often than not, the things you can change all begin with you—not with other people.

Elaine realized that she could change the way she related to her team, so she decided to increase her efforts to inspire them. Second, she committed to pacing herself so she could bring more patience and composure to the table. Both decisions led to an immediate change in the tone of the team.

But it was her third decision that made the most dramatic impact. Elaine recommitted her workweek to the things she does best: designing "drop-dead gorgeous" jewelry and working with clients. Everything else, she delegated to her new office manager.

It didn't take long to see enormous changes in her company. Within four months, every one of the underperforming team members left to pursue other jobs. As the new team developed, so did a new culture of performance and accountability. Sales reached an all-time high, and Elaine was overjoyed to feel her creative spirit come back to life.

"I had no idea how easily I could change the world around me—just by changing the way I treated everyone else. Now it makes so much sense! How can I expect others to act differently...unless I do? I was so busy complaining and worrying about what I 'should' be doing that I didn't have any energy to start creating what I really wanted!"

Her close friend Maria just laughs at this story. At 68 years young, she enjoys every day to the fullest—but it wasn't always that way: "When I was five years old, I lost a parent. Growing up, I had to take care of my brother and sister, keep the house running, and do all the things that 'should' be done. Somewhere along the way, I forgot to take care of myself and go after the things *I* wanted to do. That sure makes for a dull life.

"One day, after 60 years of drudgery, I woke up and asked myself, *'What am I doing?'* I looked around and realized I was spending my life on other people's agendas, other people's concerns, social pressures, and my family's expectations. But what about the things that are important to me? They were falling by the wayside.

"It's my life and I want to enjoy it—so I decided to! It was the best decision I ever made. Now, I'm done with 'should.' Now, I do what I want."

How old will *you* be when you step into your role of Leader of Your Life, and really make the most of what you have? The sooner you take the reins, the better your journey will be.

To speed your process along, beware of the word "should." When you hear it, stop yourself long enough to ask, *should I really? Why?*

If you get confused, ask yourself, "*Should* I do that, or do I *want* to do that?" This immediately puts the reins back in your hands, and you at choice. If the "shoulding" persists, simply smile and say, "Thank you for that suggestion." That gives you the time and space to decide for yourself if you want to follow that suggestion—or not.

If the "shoulds" in your life are coming from your own mind, make some time to examine them, one by one. Who does that "should" belong to? Whose voice is speaking? What beliefs are backing up this "should?" Keep investigating until you feel free to decide.

After all, in the end, the only person responsible for your happiness is you.

Is a Work/Life Balance Possible?

"There is only one silver bullet in life—education. That is: Learn.
Learn in school. Learn in life. Learn by
reading this book. Learn by living life."
by Rich Caccese

The author would like to acknowledge and thank his niece, Michelle, for providing a sanity check from the perspective of a 30-year-old single female who is considering going to law school...

Rich Caccese is a 50-something father and husband living in San Diego working hard on his goals to achieve a work/life balance. In addition to his family, he loves the outdoors and working on German cars. He is a project manager for the U.S. Navy, making sure that the Navy's ship propulsion systems are maintained to the right level and cost so that they can support our nation's commitments and the young sailors that man them. He is a Mechanical Engineering graduate of Penn State and bleeds blue and white, like all alumni from that terrific school. Rich can be reached at rich.caccese@yahoo.com.

The Holy Grail: balancing your work life with your personal life. I have met few people that don't want to achieve this perfect balance of having a terrific personal life with family and friends and a phenomenally successful work career. Some even think they've achieved it—until they ask their friends and family or their boss and co-workers and find out that their family and friends don't know them or why they aren't getting the promotion they want.

If you think you can achieve a work/life balance, here's an eye-opening exercise. At work, draw a circle on a clean sheet a paper. Write on top of the paper "Work Life." Now divide the circle into slices that represent the areas you need to spend your time and efforts on at work to accomplish your work goals. Such areas might include getting a graduate degree, finishing a correspondence course, reading the latest management book, attending Toastmasters to improve your public speaking skills, working two extra hours every day to keep *the* big project on track, spending an hour a day with your boss to make sure that he or she doesn't forget who you are, or…get the idea?

Size those slices to the percentage of time and effort you need to devote to each to *complete* it (not just start and then not complete it—that just adds to your stress level; if you are under a lot of stress, a good part of it is this guilty feeling you constantly have about all the things that you started but didn't finish; it's a common disease). Once you are done, put this paper away until the weekend.

Then, when you have a full day during a weekend *without* work (and that includes phone calls and emails— if you have to, "accidently" leave the Blackberry at work), pull out another clean sheet of paper and draw a similar circle with the title of "Home Life." Section the circle in the same percentages for all the things to which you want to devote your time and effort on your life outside work. These could be time at the gym, more time with your spouse, kids, and pets (or more time searching for a spouse, kid, or a pet—fish don't count), reading more books, traveling more, learn a new hobby or restarting a lost hobby, organizing your house or apartment, finding your financial files because tax season is here, well—you get the idea. Remember, it's not just the things you want to do,, but *really, truly need to do* to meet your mental image of a fulfilling life.

Women, women with children at home, and single mothers have priorities and challenges that few men truly understand. Corporate America still fails miserably at understanding and adjusting to these. This makes it extremely difficult for women, especially those with the hardest job in the world – being single Moms. Making your choices will seem like they are driven by your children and family than by yourself. But they are a part of you and when it comes to young children that rely so much on their parents (and, with single Moms, their mothers), your circle will most likely be dominated by them. There's nothing wrong with that, but consider relooking at the circle if it is all about your family and nothing about you. If it is, do two circles – one for you and one for your family. Then combine them into one circle – keeping what's most important for you intact.

Okay—once you are done with that circle, pull out the Work Life circle you made earlier in the week about work and lay the two beside each other. Spend some time crossing out any section that, after some more thought, you can throw overboard and still achieve both your work goals and a fulfilling life outside of work. This step is important— spend serious, quiet time and think through this. What is it that you really *want* to keep or really *need* to keep? Ask both the *want* and *need* questions—one represents your desires and the other, your responsibilities. They both make up who you are.

Now for the next step—and it will help if you have a well-stocked liquor cabinet for this step—did you eliminate 50 percent from your Work Life circle? Did you eliminate 50 percent from your Home Life circle? See the point here: we treat each circle as 100 percent of our time and efforts when we have only 100 percent to devote to *both* circles. The two circles combined *have to* add up to the 100 percent. There is not 200% or even 150 percent of your time and effort available; just as there aren't 28 hours in the day or nine days in the week.

If you did eliminate 50 percent of each circle, gather your family, friends, and co-workers and head out to your favorite restaurant to celebrate! If you didn't, well, that's why the liquor cabinet is important. I'm willing to bet our nation's restaurant and liquor industries on the outcome of this exercise – everyone wants to stuff 10 pounds of stuff in a 5 pound bag.

A perfect work/life balance doesn't exist. It's something just about everyone wants to achieve, some even demand it, yet it's something I have never seen accomplished. It's just not a 50–50 balance.

Most people that I have worked with fall into one of two extremes—those who put their personal life ahead of their work life and either don't achieve their work goals or set their work goals pretty low to keep their personal lives primary (a few), and those who give up on most of their personal life to achieve their work goals (the majority).

So what is going on here? Isn't the work/life balance important? Why can't it be achieved? Why do you have to sacrifice either your work or your personal life? Why can't you have it all? As much as I would like it to be, the working world is just not set up for this. And it goes beyond whoever designed the calendar for a five-day workweek and a two-day weekend (already not balanced—and, in case you didn't know, in a lot of countries it's a six-day work week and a one-day weekend). My father easily worked a 12-hour day for those five days and another six hours most Saturdays. He was a successful small business owner who always said that since he was his own boss, he didn't have to ask anyone to take time off—then he rarely took any time off! (I used to think that retirement was the compensation for working long hours like this, but Dad didn't retire until he was 73, and then he still worked a couple of hours every day for another 10 years...)

The generation that is in charge of most companies today is used to working long hours and their companies' cultures instill this expectation in their employees. Although there are some notable exceptions out there in some very progressive companies, they are rare. If you work for one of those companies, consider yourself lucky! But for the 99 percent of the rest of you, companies expect long hours and will promote those that they see having that work/life balance thing well unbalanced toward the work side.

There are some that choose a nine-to-five job purposely so that it would not affect their home life (they are the rare ones that when asked "what do you do," say something about their home life instead of their current work title like just about everyone else). They tend to get a bad rap, as many perceive a link between those that choose this with lower education. I think that's bunk—there are plenty of well-educated persons who are like the wind at 5 p.m. on a workday. But I'm sure there is research to support this position (and research that doesn't, as there is research that supports just about any socioeconomic position that someone wants to argue).

Corporate expectations for women in their fields are that those who reach the pinnacle of their fields do it at the sacrifice of family and children. Wow, is that screwed up. It's one of those cultural expectations that are changing way too slow, but it's there and dealing with it is an extremely difficult and personal challenge. Women (again, especially single moms) are seen as willing to shortchange their careers when they have to stay home with sick children or leave early to get their kids to their sports. I know of no methods to change this expectation, even ones that involved using sledgehammers to sides of managers' heads. But there are some companies with "family friendly" policies and, more importantly, enlightened managers that do not accept that a woman's career and woman having a family can't exist together. Seek those companies and bosses out when you can.

If you are reading this book, you are most likely looking to be the best in whatever field you are pursuing and long work hours are the norm for you. You want to make a difference in your chosen field; it's a basic drive for all of us.

And it doesn't matter which field you chose. I have a good friend who is a mechanic. He's one of those with a "lower education," but he's very good at his job and makes a decent living to support his two daughters (his wife works, too). I trust him with my car and my wallet (which these days, are the same thing…). He typically works between 9 and 10 hours a day and every Wednesday, he works 14 to 16 hours on his customers' cars. He simply couldn't have achieved the career success that he has as he turns 40 if he didn't put in this level of effort.

The closest I have seen to anyone achieving true work/life balance is in those who work for 30 years with virtually no life, then take early retirement to start the life part. That works for some if they maintain their health after retirement, especially if they never married or married but do not have any children. But that's probably not the math most of us were hoping for.

How about the opposite—emphasizing the Home Life circle at the beginning of your work career and then, after you turn 35, getting serious about your Work Life circle? There's definitely a lot of literature today claiming that this is now the common path that our society is following (see my comment above about research). If you believe that and then read Tom Brokaw's *The Greatest Generation* about my father's generation, who succeeded with the immense challenges of the Great Depression and World War II, you would conclude that my generation and everyone that followed this "greatest generation" are a bunch of slackers. Not true. We *are* lucky because that "greatest generation" performed extreme sacrifices to end both the world crises in the way that they did. Follow-on generations have been fortunate enough not to have to rise to the same extreme challenges. We need to give thanks for this while knowing that our generations *can* rise to those challenges if and when they come.

I know this from my own accomplishments. When I was in my 20s (married but no children), I put in the long hours just like my father did and I got recognized for it. I had 11 people working for me by the age of 27. I had gained an immeasurable amount of experience that made me what I am today in my 50s, and that I wouldn't have gotten if I didn't dive into my career as much as I did between 25 and 35.

Still don't agree? Take a look at the 1960s. John F. Kennedy's extraordinary vision of putting a man on the moon and returning him safely made the Apollo astronauts world famous. Their ages ranged from 36 to 47, with the average being 40 years old. *But* the average age of the men in Mission Control that supported them: *25* years old!

How about the current generation? I work for the United States Navy and am continually amazed (and renewed) when I see such things as an aircraft carrier launching sortie after sortie at night with both male and female sailors ensuring that the planes launch and land safely. The flight deck of an aircraft carrier at night is the most dangerous place in the world—and the average age of these sailors is *22*. There's no "slacker generation" here.

Okay—so where are we on the work/life balance? Everyone wants it. No one has it. And no one is slacking off on the work end of it. So is the only give in the home life end?

Not the answer you wanted to hear, right? Not the one I want to hear, either. In fact, not only don't I want to hear it, I refuse to accept that the only way forward is to sacrifice my home life. I know that when I'm in my final stages of life at a ripe old age (yes, I'm an optimist), I won't be thinking "I'm sure glad I spent those weeks in Norfolk, Virginia attending that work seminar instead of home in San Diego watching my son's Little League game."

Now that you think I painted you into a corner with no solution to get out, here's where I tell you the only solution that I know. In fact, unless you are independently wealthy, I'm convinced that this is the *only* solution. And it's really hard work.

Take the Work Life and Home Life circles and move them out of the way. Grab another clean sheet of paper and draw a circle. Put the title "LIFE" in really *big* letters at the top of the page. Then section off the circle, in percentages, of what you want to do in *both* Work and Home *this year*. Don't put down winning the Nobel Prize, but taking the foundation steps that you need to accomplish this year to win the Nobel Prize sometime in the future. If it helps you, break down what you want to spend your time and resources on in categories such as career, health, finance, personal growth (that's yours, not someone else's—as much as he or she needs it), relationship, free time (again, yours), and community service. Don't lock in on a even 50/50 work/life split. Find the right ratio that *fits you*. It probably isn't a perfect 50/50 and it will vary from year to year. But it's yours – take ownership of it, match it with your annual goals, and *make it happen!*

The act of doing this will focus your body, mind, and spirit on what *you* want to accomplish and let that define whatever work/life balance you end up projecting. Having just started this process a few years ago, I can tell you that this is really, really hard work to do. It takes discipline, a support network, and several tries (meaning a couple of years) to get this right. And I'm still working hard to get it right.

I hope you have enjoyed reading this chapter and that you picked up on the two basic rules that I subtly sandwiched in between the humor:

- To achieve the work/life balance that *you want*, you have to set GOALS for yourself, and
- There are no easy answers—this is hard work.

If you were hoping for find a silver bullet from this chapter that would magically bring your work and life into balance, oh well. There isn't one for this. There is only *one* silver bullet in life—*education*. That's it: Learn. Learn in school. Learn in life. Learn by reading this book. *Learn by living life.*

So, align your expectations with your work/life fit (or vice-versa) – the stress reduction alone is worth it!

You Can Always Get What You Want!

"Women could be much more powerful with us, men,
if they spent more time identifying exactly what they
wanted, making the request clearly, and then sticking by
their guns, and by their gut, when they do not receive
exactly what they have asked for."
by Mitch Simon

*An executive coach with JD and MBA degrees from
UCLA, Mitch Simon has 20 years of executive experience in
strategic planning, marketing, and leadership development at
Fortune 500 companies. He coaches CEOs, VPs, C-level teams,
and executive sales teams in competitive industries such as
professional services, real estate, technology, communications,
and banking in the areas of team development, leadership
development, strategic development, and execution, and leads
powerful executive annual retreats. Clients include Morgan
Stanley, Qualcomm, Grubb & Ellis, CSC, Foley & Lardner,
Baker & McKenzie, QSC Audio Products, California Bank
& Trust, Pacific National Laboratories, Jitterbug, and CDC
Small Business Finance. Through one-on-one and team
coaching, Mitch challenges his clients to achieve greater
professional and personal achievement through provocative
conversations, raising the bar, and taking greater risks through*

developing excellence in leadership and teaming. A certified integral coach, he has taught courses in Authentic Leadership, High Performance Teams, and Fierce Conversations at USD and UCLA and has authored the book The Trusted Advocate. His primary goal is to provoke great leaders to encourage the rest of their organizations to pursue excellence both at work and at home.

I attended a wonderful workshop by Allison Armstrong, who teaches "Understanding Men." Allison mentioned that the difference between men and women is that when men say something has to be a certain way, well then, it has to be that "certain way." When women say that it has to be a certain way, they really mean that it has to be "in the ballpark."

At that moment, my decade's worth of coaching men and women all came to a culmination before my very eyes. I remember teaching a workshop to a room full of women on "The Power of No." After much reflection, I see that I had no integrity in offering that workshop. Instead, I should have spent the entire two hours supporting women in carefully addressing what they truly wanted to say *yes* to.

In my experience, women could be much more powerful with us, men, if they spent more time identifying exactly what they wanted, making the request clearly, and then sticking by their guns, and by their gut, when they do not receive exactly what they have asked for.

I believe women, as great teachers and providers, short-change the rest of us by allowing us to get away with not living in full integrity. By allowing men to not understand what women want, and then to short-change them in the delivery, cheats women out of what men truly desire and gives men permission to not live up to their full capabilities. I say it is high time that all women take action in getting the specific actions that they want from men. It is time that women learn and are skilled in what Fernando Flores calls the "Conversation for Action."

The Conversation for Action provides four phases to support women in creating powerful requests, and having men take action in exact accordance with what women desire. Becoming skillful in all four phases will allow women to not only ask for and get what they want, but learn how to get what they might not even have imagined was possible.

Below is a simple diagram that illustrates the four phases of the Conversation for Action. Every phase of the conversation has as its fulcrum the conditions of satisfaction that the woman ("customer") desires. The Conversation for Action begins with a request and does not end until the woman acknowledges that the work has been satisfactorily completed by the man ("provider").

The Conversation for Action

As an introduction, let me share the overall goal of each phase. The four quadrants in the diagram correspond to the four phases of the exchange between a woman ("customer") and a man ("provider"):

PREPARATION	**CLARIFICATION AND NEGOTIATION**
• The woman prepares her request ending in a request with specific conditions of satisfaction.	• The negotiation and clarification of the conditions of satisfaction ending in a promise
SATISFACTION	**FULFILLMENT**
• The woman's examination of the delivery, ending in a declaration of satisfaction or dissatisfaction in the form of "thank you" or "this is not what I expected"	• The completion of the promise. ending in a declaration of completion

The Preparation Phase

The source of a request derives from a woman who is concerned that something is missing. The woman begins the process of constructing the specific conditions that will satisfy her and make the woman whole and complete. This phase ends when the woman makes the formal request to the man.

Everything above sounds pretty straightforward and simple. Unfortunately, where many women go wrong is that they are so used to not getting what they want, and in fact are "okay" with not getting what they want, that they lack the discomfort that should accompany this.

The breakdowns in the Preparation Phase:

- Determining that a breakdown has occurred that you cannot take care of on your own

Many women, or let us say "superwomen," decide from an early age that they can take care of everything—I repeat, *everything*—by themselves. As a result, when breakdowns occur, they don't see them, and instead get caught in the ever-revolving circle of taking care of everything all the time.

- Is the request something out of the ordinary?

When a woman has determined that a breakdown has occurred, that in fact she wants something that she doesn't have, most women settle for something that is, well, just ordinary. Women don't always take the time to ask for what will make them delighted, not just happy.

The question I want to know the answer to is, what exactly would be extraordinary for you? What would make your heart sing? Too often the greatest issue is that women negotiate with themselves in preparing for the ask. They overthink what people will offer them, and under-express the request.

- Clarifying conditions of satisfaction

When do you want your request fulfilled? How do you want your request fulfilled? Who must fulfill your request?

The biggest breakdowns I see here come from a woman not spending the time to go to the heart and gut level as to what would truly make her satisfied.

The preparation phase ends only when the request with specific conditions of satisfaction has been communicated and received by the man. Without these two pieces, power slippages will occur throughout the "transaction."

The Clarification and Negotiation Phase

After the request is communicated to a man, the Clarification and Negotiation Phase begins. This phase is where the conditions of satisfaction are discussed, accepted "as is," modified, or declined. The Clarification and Negotiation Phase is best approached with the commitment to find out if what you want is exactly what a Provider can articulate back to you.

The breakdowns in the Negotiation Phase:

- Not taking the time to clarify the Conditions of Satisfaction to ensure there is no misunderstanding

Too many times, women walk away from the "scene of the crime" with the man saying, "Yes, I can provide this." Well, in fact, the man never really heard what the woman wanted. It is important that the woman feel completely satisfied that her request was heard, such that the man can speak the request back to her.

- Leaving the scene of the crime with a "no"

The woman should never allow the response to be a "no." The very least she should expect is a "promise to promise." A promise to promise is the man's way of saying, "I don't know today, but I promise I will get back to you at a specific date and time with an appropriate response." As someone who holds to her commitments, a woman should always look for a "promise to promise" over a no.

- Making a promise you believe you can fulfill and you are committed to fulfilling

Finally, it is extremely important that the woman know for certain that the man is speaking with the full commitment and power to fulfill the request. It is very important that when a woman asks for something, she knows that the man is sincere *and* has the competency and experience to provide what she is looking for. Only when the making of the promise has been communicated and accepted by the woman has the Negotiation and Clarification Phase been completed.

The Fulfillment Phase

During the Fulfillment Phase, the woman must make sure that the man takes the action necessary to fulfill the promise. It is here where the woman holds the man to a high standard in fully communicating progress and breakdowns and in asking for support. A woman should only work with a man who makes declarations of "completion" to her.

Common power slippages during the Fulfillment Phase:

- Not informing the woman when something is jeopardizing the promise and asking for support and changes if required

In looking for men to work with, it is incumbent upon the woman to find individuals who have nothing to hide. As a woman, make sure you work with someone who has the integrity to tell when something is not working.

- Not resolving breakdowns that occur

In searching whom to work with, you must expect that breakdowns will occur. It is important that the man you are working with is skilled in working through breakdowns. It is incumbent upon the woman to choose a man who has the skills to work through things.

- Not giving progress reports as appropriate

In asking for the extraordinary, it is important that you choose someone who is willing to share his progress. You *are* allowed and entitled to know what is happening on the man's side.

- Not declaring completion

Too often women lose power by accepting delivery without the man actually articulating that he has, in his mind, met all of a woman's conditions of satisfaction. It is imperative that the man declare that in fact he has delivered the "goods" according to all requested parameters. Only then has the third phase been completed.

The Declaration of Satisfaction Phase

There is always a gap between the "declaration of completion" and the "declaration of satisfaction." When the actions are completed and delivery is made to the woman, the woman must determine whether the results match the conditions of satisfaction. There is only one way to find out . . . the woman must ask!

Breakdowns during the Satisfaction Phase:

• Not declaring satisfaction or dissatisfaction

As the woman, *you* have the right to get what you want *and* declare whether in fact you got what you wanted. For many women, the man gets to determine whether she has been satisfied. Women, it is your satisfaction that the man is after. Demand that you are satisfied.

• Not dealing with broken promises

For many women, the problem is that they don't like to, or don't want to, deal with broken promises. As a woman, you are entitled to get everything you want and in exactly the way you want it. If a promise has been broken in the delivery of your request, you must work with the man to fulfill that promise.

• Not choosing a man who asks whether you are satisfied

You can't always get what you want; however, you can always work with someone who cares whether in fact you are satisfied. As you can see from this lengthy process to achieve what your heart desires, it is very important to choose a man who is committed to delivering on your requests. It is important that you stay committed to your commitments and the commitments of the man, so much so that you find only those men who will go the last mile to not only deliver what you want, but who care that you are completely satisfied.

Conclusion

Many of the breakdowns I have encountered in working with women occur because they are not committed enough to their commitments to choose people, providers, or companies that are in alignment with their desires. Ladies, you are always teaching people how to treat you. Whenever you decide there is something that you want, make it big, and choose men who want to make you completely happy. There are plenty of us out there.